MAKING RUSTIC FURNITURE

MAKING RUSTIC FURNITURE

DANIEL MACK

A Sterling/Lark Book
Sterling Publishing Co., Inc.   New York

Published in 1992 by Lark Books
50 College Street
Asheville, North Carolina, U.S.A., 28801

Editor: Eric Carlson
Art Director: Marcia Winters
Production: Elaine Thompson, Sandra Montgomery, Marcia Winters

ISBN 0-8069-8264-0

Library of Congress Cataloging-in-Publication Data

Mack, Daniel.
        Making rustic furniture / by Daniel Mack.
            p.   cm.
        "A Sterling/Lark book."
        Includes bibliographical references and index.
        ISBN 1-887374-12-4
        1. Furniture making.   2. Country furniture.   I. Title.
    TT194.M3 1990
    684.1'042—dc20   90-4517
                                                         CIP

Photos of contemporary furniture were contributed by the makers except where
noted. Photos of Daniel Mack, his furniture, and projects are by Bobby Hansson.
Other photos and sources include: Clarence O. Nichols and his work, courtesy of
the New York State Museum, Albany, NY; John Krubsack, State Historical Society of
Wisconsin; Ernest Stowe sideboard, Adirondack Museum, Blue Mountain Lake, NY;
Lee Fountain table, Jim Swedburg; Tom Phillips' work, Judy Phillips. Photos: Page 14
(bottom), M. A. Tupling; Pgs 16 (bottom), 37, 40, Lynne Reynolds; Pgs 18 (bottom),
39, Gene Gouss; Pgs 43, 44, 48, 49, 56, Laird Monteith; Pg 70 (top) Kenro Izu,
(bottom) Alex Casler; Pg 71, Frontispiece, Kenro Izu. Cover photo by Jim Erwin.
Cover background photo by Evan Bracken.

Photos and illustrations for the "Rustic Arbor" project appeared in *Fine Gardening*
magazine (subscriptions available at $24 per year from The Taunton Press, 63 South
Main St., Box 5506, Newtown, CT 06470).

Printed in Hong Kong by
Oceanic Graphic Printing

CONTENTS

ACKNOWLEDGEMENTS

Like a first rustic chair, this book took much longer than expected. There were many people who provided support at crucial times. My wife Teri Mack learned to live with and care for this project that just moved in on us like a frisky puppy. This book reflects her patience, insight, and stamina.

Rustic makers all over the country were enthusiastic and responsive to my call for information and photos. We used as many photos as possible. But pictures of some interesting work, for reasons of space or photo quality, did not make it into this book. I appreciate all the cooperation by my fellow rusticks as well as the hundred students over the past few years whose inventiveness never ceased to amaze me.

There are people who provided the many twists and turns that made the rustic story more interesting: The librarians at the Strong Museum in Rochester, New York, were scouting material for me for a few years. Mary K. Darrah of New Hope, Pennsylvania, added important historical and European elements. Lynda Moss at the Western Heritage Center in Billings, Montana, introduced me to much of the western rustic style.

This book would never have been done without a supportive group of book people. Rob Pulleyn, publisher at Lark Books, took a chance and leapt into an unknown project and stayed with it. The editor, Eric Carlson, was masterful at understanding the spirit of the book. He magnified it and preserved it throughout the constraints of production. Marsha Melnick and Susan Meyer of Roundtable Press offered needed counsel and encouragement. Finally Bobby Hansson, whose photos comprise the bulk of this book, did double service as the designer/mechanic behind many of the projects. His long experience with book photography, his dedication to crafts and the rustic way, and his friendship with me, guided and leavened this project in uncounted ways.

—Daniel Mack

INTRODUCTION: A RUSTIC ODYSSEY

There is something immediately familiar about rustic furniture. Even if you have never seen it before and the idea of a chair made from trees is shocking, you understand it. That recognition is a big part of our enduring fascination with rustic furniture. The tree, the chair, the tree...you see the connection and some deep, sleepy part of your mind stirs. You want to look, you want to touch, maybe you want to make. This book is about all these things.

The first time I remember seeing rustic furniture was in 1978 at Deetjen's Big Sur Inn in Big Sur, California. There were two pieces of redwood, joined together, gently forming seats. I was so intrigued by this clash of nature and human utility that I sat and sketched what I saw.

Looking at the drawings now, after ten years of building my own rustic chairs, I recognize the cooperative quality of these chairs. They are both chairs and trees at the same time. Neither the function nor the material has dominated. That ambiguity is part of their beauty.

There was something else about those chairs that seems to have lingered with me. They were well-chosen bits of the forest that had been placed in a human setting. They weren't meant to be sculptures or model trees or examples of "redwood." They were simply natural mementos, carefully selected, minimally transformed, and unpretentiously placed for people to sit on.

During the following year I began to notice older twig pieces at auctions and yard sales. In 1979, just after my first daughter was born, I bought a little hickory child's chair. It had been left out in the elements and had begun to deteriorate. But enough of its strength and beauty remained to make it still a durable chair.

I replaced the broken splint seat with blue Shaker tape. What I admired about my stick chair was its texture. That bark, which had once protected the young saplings, was now protecting the chair, lending natural history to this little piece of furniture.

That summer I was spending weekends in the Catskill Mountains a few hours north of New York City. I was surrounded by maple trees: big trees, old trees, and their next generations—lots of scrubby "volunteer saplings"—all twisting toward the light. I had absolutely never built anything, ever: no soap box derby cars, no birdhouses, certainly no tree houses. I was by no means "handy." Nonetheless, into my mind crept an outrageous thought: "Perhaps I could build a twig chair..."

No one would have to know. I could do it in the barn. I could burn my mistakes. I grabbed a saw and cut a few trees. I got a drill, an axe, a knife, some glue, and I was off. I used my little auction chair to copy the proportions, to replace the straight, chunky pieces of hickory with spiny, delicate pieces of maple.

The first half-dozen such chairs are gone now, unrecorded. They tipped forward. They looked ultra-primitive. Perhaps the axe was too crude and mean a tool for making good joints. The wood was too green and it shrunk in the wrong places. But the proportions live on in the child's chairs I build even now.

I couldn't stop building chairs. My Manhattan apartment became my first workshop, cluttered with bundles of sticks drying in the corner of the living room. Then somehow my wife and I thought it would be a good idea if the bedroom became a workshop, so we moved into the living room. More chairs, more sticks.

As my life began to revolve more and more around stick furniture, I discovered an old tintype of my grandfather Cornelius Mack as a young man, sitting on a spiny twig bench in some photographer's studio. I had had this picture for at least fifteen years and maybe longer. But it suddenly took on a new meaning and importance.

In 1983 I set up my first studio. It was four hundred square feet in a rented loft in Harlem, about fifteen minutes from home. There I built more chairs. I tried making a bed, then some tables, and I began to realize that any furniture could be made from sticks. Each new discovery

Below:
Maple child's chair, 1981

Below right:
Cornelius Mack and friend, c. 1904

brought new questions as I struggled and experimented with proportions, seating, finishing, and good joinery.

I began with the idea that a chair is only as strong as its joints. So, I reasoned, if my joints are only 5/8" in diameter, the pieces of my chairs don't have to be much bigger than that. This thought, right or wrong, allowed me to experiment with the proportions of chairs, trying to find the relationship between the size of the posts and the size of the rungs that would give the chair...magic.

Magic? In a piece of furniture? It's an elusive quality of rustic work that allows a chair to look and work like a chair while still retaining the grace and variety of the tree itself. In search of this magic, I came to see that each species of tree has a different growth style: Some curve more than others. Some are straight as they push

Below left:
Maple side chair
with rope seat, 1981

Below right:
Maple arm chair
with woven leather
seat, 1981

toward the sunlight and twist with the seasons. Different forest conditions effect tree growth: Thick forests, hillside forests, wetland forests—all produce different styles of trees.

Above all, I wanted to retain the animated energy of the tree in my chairs. The old hickory child's chair is static. It just sits there, like a pleasant rustic object. I wanted to create chairs that looked like flash-frozen tree dancers. I wanted legs that kicked, backs that bent, arms that embraced.

As I spent more time in the woods, I came to discover the odd trees, the ones that were losing their fight for survival. They had been gnawed by deer, attacked by bugs, nicked by passing snowmobiles. Some had been blown over, some knocked over. These are the distressed trees that have their own kind of energy. They talk more of decay and impermanence than of vitality and strength. I began to use these trees in my chairs.

On some of the trees I collected, the bark fell off. At one point, in 1984, I had enough such pieces to build a chair. It had a very different feeling. The natural shape was there, but the texture had changed. Gone were the earthy, leathery browns. Now there was an

Children's chairs, maple, 1984

ivory, bone look. These chairs were more elegant, more cool, more "civilized," some people said. Getting further into the tree—just beneath the bark—got me further out of the woods and the forest. The resulting pieces had left the "country" and became more "citified." I did many, many of these peeled-maple chairs. I still do them.

Maple arm chair with bird's nest, 1988

I consider myself primarily a chairmaker, using spare, natural forms. For me, a successful rustic chair looks like a particular person made this particular chair from a few particular trees. A good rustic chair is like the transcript of a conversation between a person and a tree. Both the chairmaker and the tree are recognizable in the final result. It is an authored celebration of the form and beauty marks of a tree. The tree is no longer wild in the woods, nor has it become lumber.

The maker is not a carpenter, imposing a plan on wood, nor is he a nurseryman, relocating trees. The tree and the maker have collaborated. A successful rustic chair has life. It has the life of the tree and the spirit of the maker. The combination of the branches retain the swaying, twisting grace of the tree. The result is animation: A chair that seems as if it could move. A chair that makes you feel as if it just might walk around the room when you leave.

A successful rustic chair has grace. In Greek mythology, the Graces were three daughters of Zeus who spread joy in the world of nature. The joy of a rustic piece comes first from the simple fact of its existence; secondly from the way it echoes the shapes and textures of nature; and thirdly from the unique way in which a particular piece combines the elements of a tree into a

Photo: M. A. Tupling

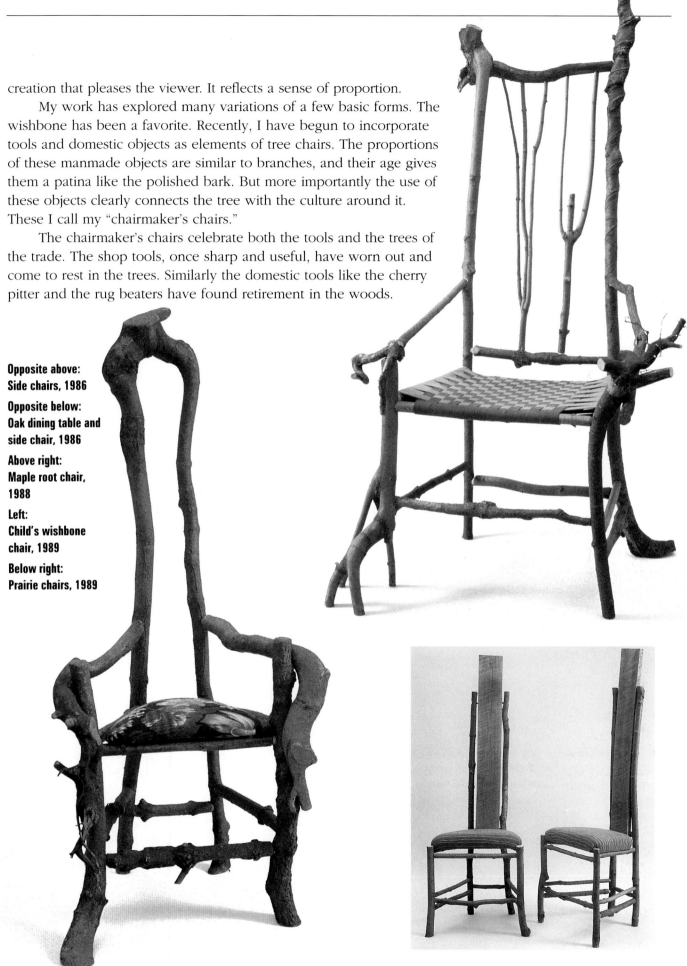

creation that pleases the viewer. It reflects a sense of proportion.

My work has explored many variations of a few basic forms. The wishbone has been a favorite. Recently, I have begun to incorporate tools and domestic objects as elements of tree chairs. The proportions of these manmade objects are similar to branches, and their age gives them a patina like the polished bark. But more importantly the use of these objects clearly connects the tree with the culture around it. These I call my "chairmaker's chairs."

The chairmaker's chairs celebrate both the tools and the trees of the trade. The shop tools, once sharp and useful, have worn out and come to rest in the trees. Similarly the domestic tools like the cherry pitter and the rug beaters have found retirement in the woods.

Opposite above:
Side chairs, 1986

Opposite below:
Oak dining table and side chair, 1986

Above right:
Maple root chair, 1988

Left:
Child's wishbone chair, 1989

Below right:
Prairie chairs, 1989

Above left:
First peeled maple
chair, 1983

Above right:
Peeled fork chair,
1991
Metropolitan Home
Show house

Below: Split-grain
dining chairs, table,
1986

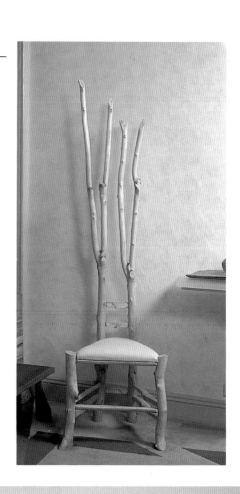

Photo: Lynne Reynolds

Below:
Peeled maple wishbone, 1986

Right:
Peeled maple wishbone settee, 1987

Below right:
Peeled maple arm chair, 1985

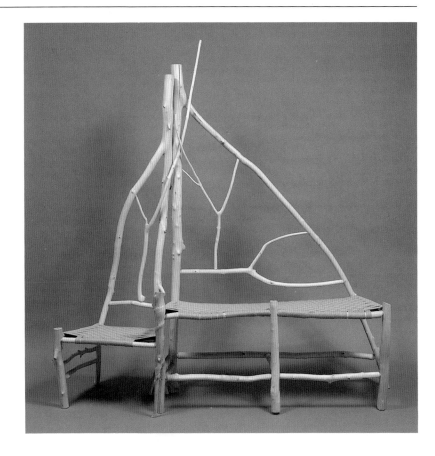

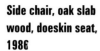

Side chair, oak slab wood, doeskin seat, 1986

Side chair, maple, 1987

Maple side chairs, oak table, 1988

Photo: Gene Gouss

"Chairmaker's
Chair," 1989

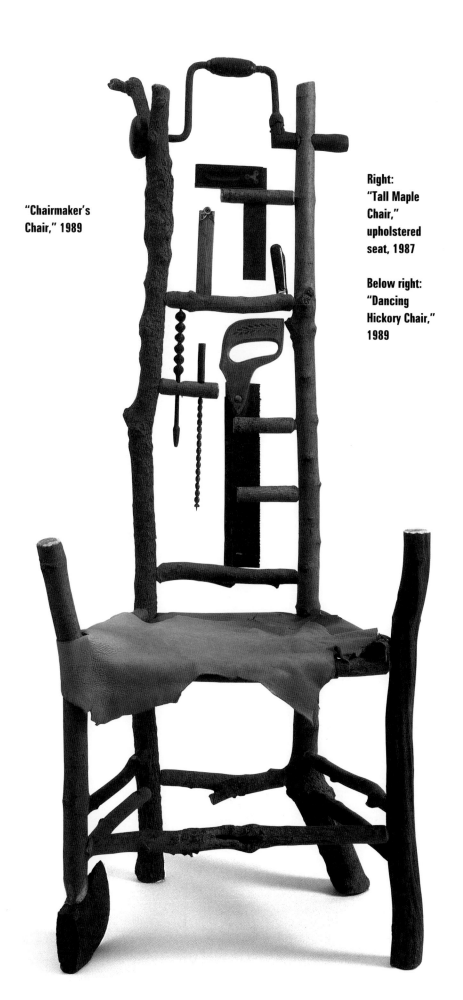

Right:
"Tall Maple
Chair,"
upholstered
seat, 1987

Below right:
"Dancing
Hickory Chair,"
1989

1.

LOOKING AT RUSTIC FURNITURE

WAYS OF LOOKING AT RUSTIC FURNITURE

There are hundreds of people who are building or have built rustic furniture. Describing this furniture and its makers is as easy—and difficult—as describing trees themselves. The easy way is to call a tree a tall woody plant and to call rustic furniture the things made from tall woody plants. The makers are people who make furniture from tall woody plants.

A more complicated description involves pondering the variations in the trees, the furniture, and the makers themselves. Rustic furniture is linked to history and creative innovation. It has roots in the infinite diversity of climate and terrain, with branches extending into business, recreation, and repaired lives.

Rustic furniture is regional furniture. Its form and composition varies with the distribution and availability of trees around the world. For instance, there aren't sugar maples in Colorado, so when I teach classes at a crafts center in Snowmass, they ask that I send a load of Eastern maples so I can teach with the woods I know best.

Colorado makers Margaret Craven, Paul Ries, and others work with aspen, scrub oak, willow and other locally grown trees. California maker Michael Emmons works with eucalyptus. Californian Micki Voisard uses manzanita. Adirondack builder Tom Phillips uses white and golden birch. Oregon maker Brent McGregor uses juniper. Kansas maker Bud Hanzlick builds from Osage orange, a wood that farmers consider to be a weed.

Rustic furniture can be built from any wood. But what gives the furniture an extra-special quality is that it's built from a particular

RUSTIC GREATNESS
By Robert E. Doyle

The first time I encountered a truly great example of Adirondack rustic furniture was in the late spring of 1967. I was alone, fishing a private lake in the central Adirondacks, when it began to rain heavily. I ran for the shelter of a covered porch attached to a vacant summer lodge. There were several rocking chairs scattered about the length of the porch, and pushed against the inside wall was a small table.

At first, I saw only a stump-base end table, extremely graceful in form and perfectly proportioned. But it seemed so organic, so full of expected movement, that it somehow demanded closer scrutiny. The top of the table was rectangular with truncated corners and skirted edges. Its surface was covered with tiny split twigs arranged in a tight geometric pattern that would expand and contract as I looked at it, dazzling the eye with its design.

I was in awe of this table. It seemed to reveal itself in layers. When I stepped back to look again at the complete form, I noticed the support braces: limb-like, arranged and scaled to flow naturally from stump to table top. Bending to examine the base, I found another layer of craft and design. The stump had also been partially veneered with wood in a particular area. As you look at contemporary rustic furniture, try to identify its origin by the type of woods used. You'll find that rustic furniture is truly rooted in the land.

CONTEMPORARY STYLES OF RUSTIC FURNITURE

Within each region, each style of rustic furniture is being passed through the minds and hands of makers living in these last years of the twentieth century. None of the builders I know is strictly "reproducing" old rustic designs. All are aware of other contemporary work through exhibitions, galleries, and magazines. They are also familiar with historical rustic pieces documented in such books as Craig Gilborn's *Adirondack Furniture and the Rustic Tradition*, Sue Honaker Stephenson's *Rustic Furniture* and Susan Osborn's *American Rustic Furniture*.

Contemporary rustic furniture can be roughly categorized by some of its design characteristics. There seem to be about seven major "styles," although makers frequently combine more than one of these techniques in their work. There are also a number of interesting variations of rustic work which use unusual materials or techniques in a rustic manner.

In addition to examples of contemporary work in each of these styles, I have included some unique historical materials that may be helpful in understanding contemporary rustic work. Finally, the reader is encouraged to refer ahead in the book to hands-on projects in each style.

split twigs arranged in interconnecting lanes of geometric pattern.

This table was fascinating sculpture, obviously crafted by a master woodworker who understood rustic materials, cabinetwork, and the marriage of form to function. The builder had complete control of his creation, yet he never constrained its energy in any way. It was art. It was craft. It displayed technical knowledge. And it was useful.

When evaluating a piece of rustic furniture, it should first be considered as art. Look at the form, the textures, the tone, and the design. Do these elements exponentially compound the design as a whole, rather than simply adding components? Does the piece seem to stand still and move at the same time? Does it please and entertain your eye?

Next, examine the craftsmanship and technical knowledge demonstrated in the piece. Is the joinery solid, unobtrusive, and integral to the whole object? Did the maker choose rustic material suited to its intended purpose and well-fitted in scale and relationship to the other parts of the object?

Finally, if it is to be a piece of furniture, you must ask yourself: Is it useful? Does it meet your needs?

If a piece of rustic furniture successfully meets all these criteria, it can be considered truly great.

STICK

Stick or sapling furniture is made from small trees and branches, joined in a manner that mimics the way they grew. The maker's art is in the way the wood is selected and combined into beautiful and functional furniture.

More than any other rustic work, stick style is intuitive, spontaneous, and interactive. Usually there are very few plans to be followed, just a few interesting sticks to be combined. The maker must remain flexible and be willing to make ongoing changes during the building as each added element suggests new possibilities.

Stick style often seems insubstantial. People associate sticks with those things that break under your feet while walking in the woods. That's kindling—dry wood that has begun to decay and return to the earth. To the rustic builder, sticks are strong pieces of wood, cut fresh and dried. They have the strength of lumber and the illusion of frailty.

Stick chairs are like pencil-line drawings of trees. Some of us build from crooked sticks, others prefer straight sticks. Some peel their sticks. Some leave the bark on. Some makers nail their sticks together. Some use glued mortise-and-tenon joints. Others fasten with dowels. But in general, all use small trees and branches, combined in a manner that echoes the proportions of natural growth.

Garden table and chairs, willow, Liz Sifrit Hunt, OH

Stick chairs, settee,
and barstool, Brad
Greenwood, CA

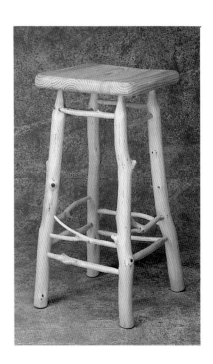

Right:
Osage orange
settee, Bud
Hanzlick, KS

Below:
Maple side chair,
Daniel Mack, NY

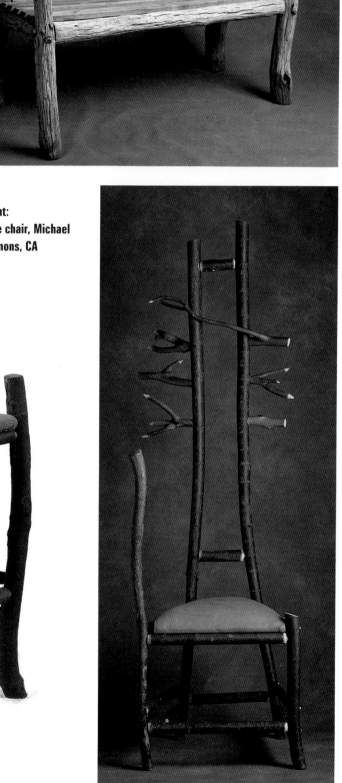

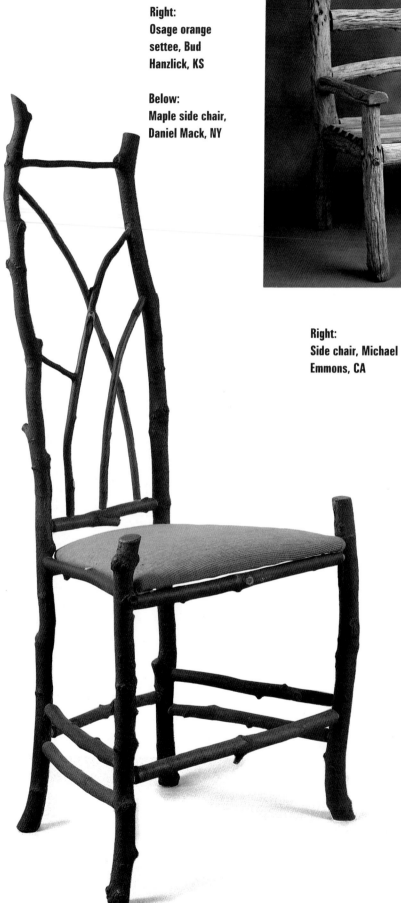

Right:
Side chair, Michael
Emmons, CA

**Table, settee,
and side chairs,
Michael Emmons, CA**

Left:
Maple arm chairs, Daniel Mack, NY

Right:
Chair and table, willow, Michael Emmons, CA

Below left:
Side chair, Michael Emmons, CA

Below right:
Table with rug, Lillian Dodson, NY

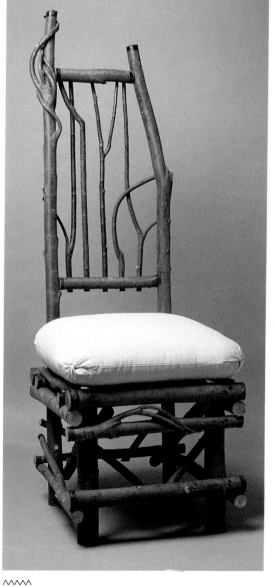

Below:
Chair, Lillian
Dodson, NY

Right:
Willow cube
tables, Michael
Emmons, CA

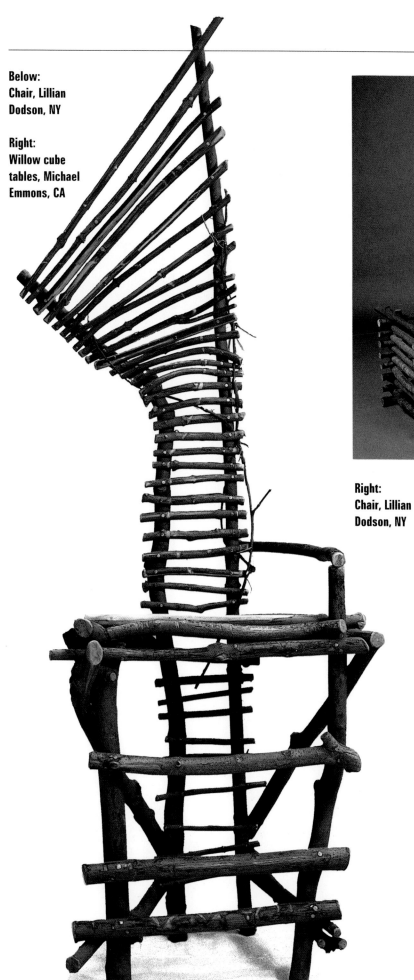

Right:
Chair, Lillian
Dodson, NY

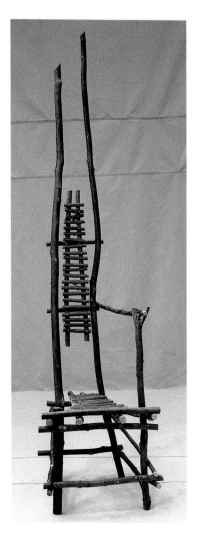

Right:
Reconstructed
side chair,
Daniel Mack, NY

Below:
Peeled and
gouged manzanita
grouping, Micki
Voisard, CA

Below:
Willow coffee table,
Michael Emmons, CA

Right:
Rocker, mixed
woods, Barry
Gregson, NY

Below:
Settee, mixed
hardwoods, Barry
Gregson, NY

RUSTIC
TRADITIONS

Of all the rustic furniture
styles, contemporary stick
makers have the widest
variety of historical influences on which to draw.
Superb collections have been
preserved, photographed,
and documented, especially
in the Adirondack Mountain
region of upstate New York,
where rustic building was a
necessary response to life in
a remote locale. One such
"rustic character" was
Clarence Nichols, who completed a dining table and six
of these chairs in 1947.
See page 84.

Top left:
Settee, maple and slate, Don King, CO

Top right:
Wishbone maple chair, Daniel Mack, NY

Below left:
Garden settee, David Robinson, NY

Below right:
Planter, Margaret Craven, CO

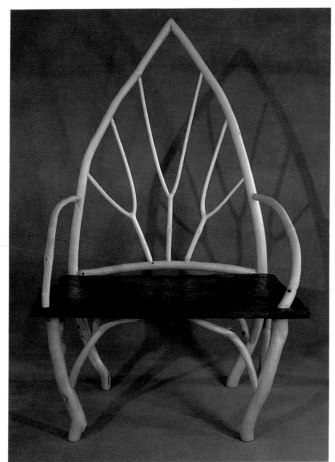

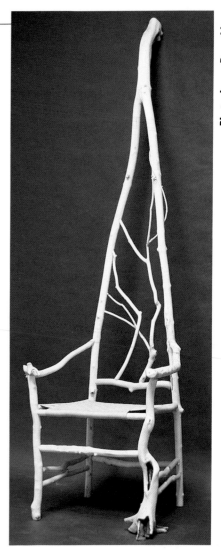

Photo: Lynne Reynolds

Right:
Nailed willow
settee, Elaine Shay,
Liz Sifrit Hunt, OH

Below left:
Manzanita arm
chair, Micki Voisard,
CA

Below right:
Manzanita side
chair, Micki Voisard,
CA

Right:
Birch camelback
settee, Grants, NY

Below left:
Nailed willow side
chair, Michael
Emmons, CA

Below right:
Wishbone
children's chairs,
Daniel Mack, NY

Photo: Gene Gouss

Below:
Side chair, ironwood
and metal rods,
Chris Anna, NY

Right:
Nailed willow side
table, Michael
Emmons, CA

Below right:
Arm chair, Michael
Emmons, CA

TREES AND LOGS

Tree work or log work furniture is basically just big stick furniture. Here the large limbs or sections of trunks are used as structural elements. The furniture is substantial in look and weight and may have a few natural curves or bends. Its shape is constructed. Cedar logs are popular in the Adirondacks. In the West, it's lodgepole pine, aspen, or juniper. Log work is used where there is enough space to adequately frame the large proportions of the pieces.

For indoor furniture, any type of log will work. But for outdoor projects, certain woods hold up better than others. Black locust, white cedar, and redwood are resistant woods that work very well outdoors. The logs are usually peeled to minimize the possibility of bug infestation. I do primarily interior work so my log of choice is white cedar, which has very little weight for its volume, making the finished prod-

**Canopy bed,
juniper table,
Brent McGregor, OR**

uct easier to move. White cedar is also easy to work and finish.

Tree work furniture is more of a house-builder's trade than a chairmaker's art. Often tree work furniture is built into the house. The size, weight, and growth pattern of the elements limit the options for lyrical, animated work. The feel of log work pieces is permanent and immoveable.

In addition to furniture, log workers build gazebos, pergolas, arbors, and other outdoor rustic structures. The traditional work in New York's Central Park and at the Mohonk Mountain House in the lower Catskill Mountains of New York State has had a strong historical influence on log builders. Also, the rustic log style is the official architecture of the U.S. National Parks. Yellowstone Lodge and the lodge at Mt. Hood are conspicuous examples. Some log or tree work resembles oversized stick work. Other log workers use roots and burls, which add curves and rounded forms to the otherwise straight-line designs.

Log and maple bed, pickled white, Daniel Mack, NY

**Settee,
Brent McGregor, OR**

**Stairway,
David Robinson, NY**

Arch settee, bridge,
and gazebo, David
Robinson, NY

Left: Gazebo, David Robinson, NY

Right: Juniper bed, Brent McGregor, OR

Below: Cedar and maple loft, Daniel Mack, NY

RUSTIC TRADITIONS

Decorative outdoor log work was a logical extension of the frontier home, where logs were used as a basic building component and for just about anything that called for sturdy construction. The outdoor log structures in New York City's Central Park inspired wealthy city dwellers to borrow the rustic style for their mountain camps. This early 1900s postcard depicts an imaginative use of logs for a park gate in Sacandaga, New York.

Top:
Bed, Brad
Greenwood, CA

Above: Entrance gate, Ausable Club, NY

Entrance to Park, Sacandaga Park, N. Y.

BENTWOOD

Bentwood furniture is made by bending and nailing long, straight, fresh branches or suckers of trees around a frame. Unlike most stick work, bentwood furniture is carefully planned before it is made. Usually the plan and the finished piece are similar. This style of rustic is often made by family groups, where any and all family members can participate.

Bent willow furniture, commonly made in the southern United States, is one of the best-known styles. There are families throughout the South making designs of bentwood furniture that have been handed down for generations. The Amish—throughout Pennsylvania, western New York, Ohio, and Indiana—build another distinctive form of bentwood furniture that combines naturally formed wood and milled wood in the same chairs. There are many individuals building in this style throughout the United States, wherever there are supple, fast-growing woods, such as willow, alder, or cottonwood.

Bentwood chair, Greg Adams, IN

**Bent willow chair,
Clifton Montieth, MI**

**Bent willow settee
and table, Monte
Lindsley, WA**

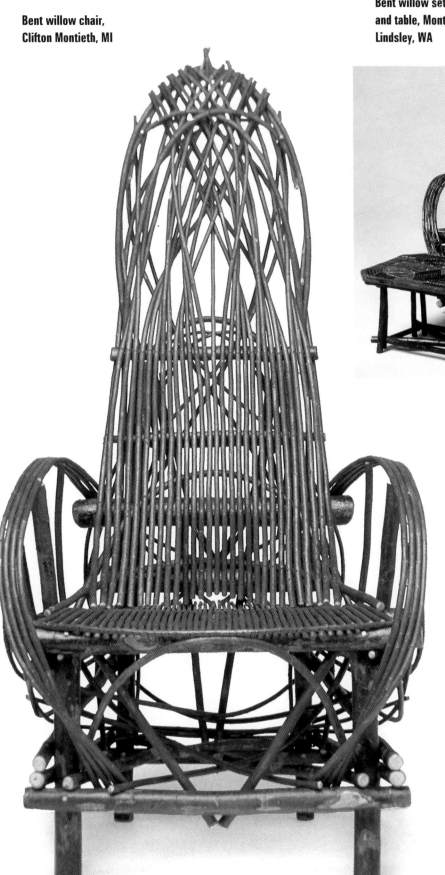

**Bent willow chair,
Clifton Monteith, MI**

Right:
Willow table, Clifton
Montieth, MI

Below left:
Bent willow chair,
Michael Emmons, CA

Below right:
Bent willow chair,
Michael Emmons, CA

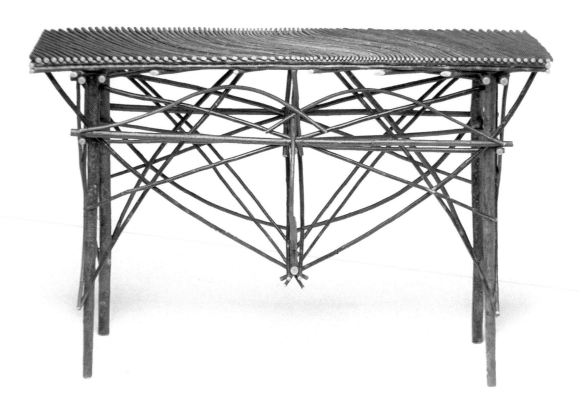

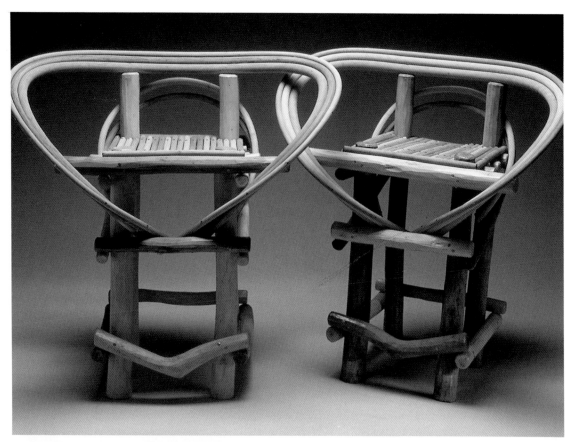

Left:
Colored bentwood chairs, Barry Schwartz, NY

Below left:
Bentwood chair, Barry Schwartz, NY

Below right:
Bent willow settee, Michael Emmons, CA

WILLOW DESIGNS
by Michael Emmons

I have been making rustic furniture, using river willow, since 1979. Before this, I had been a goldsmith. I was working small, using a different material, a different method. The change was as disparate as fire is to water. Each tree, each branch, has a different shape, a different message. Each piece whispers, guides the hand. In a way, a chair helps to build itself.

Green wood has possibilities and presents problems that rigid, seasoned wood doesn't have. Willow is a supple material that can be manipulated into a curved, flowing design. The pliancy of the wood is dependent upon the moisture within the fiber.

My first chair began as a personal project. I simply wanted to make a chair for our house that would be comfortable. As a model, I used a battered and deformed old willow chair my brother had made. Although I was very proud of my first effort, it was best suited for a potted philodendron. During the next several attempts, I became more aware of the special relationships that go into making a comfortable chair.

Finally, I made a willow chair that I was happy with and I was thoroughly infected with the desire to continue making willow furniture. The sweet, green branches felt so good in my hands. They were alive. I could bend them into an object that was both beautiful and functional. I felt as though I were working with wands of light.

I began to apply the principles of ergonomics to other designs. I was now concerned with making each chair comfortable. I developed a loveseat, several rocker designs, dining chairs, dining tables, a chaise lounge, straight-backed chairs, coffee tables, headboards, room dividers. The possibilities had expanded.

For the chairs to be complete, they needed cushions. My wife, Ronna, who is a fine artist,

began experimenting with fabric designs and cushion possibilities. She finally settled on a fluffy, dacron-filled, inner cushion with a removable slipcover. She painted the material for the slipcovers with abstract scenes and reflections of the areas where willows grow. There is a natural relationship in the way her designs complement the design of the furniture.

Left:
Bent willow settee, Paula
Moody, Barry Jones, GA

Upper right:
"The Victorian," Paula
Moody, Barry Jones, GA

Lower left:
Bent willow settee,
Michael Emmons, CA

Lower right:
Bent willow chair,
Michael Emmons, CA

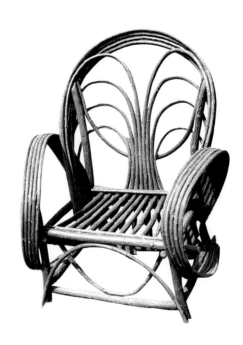

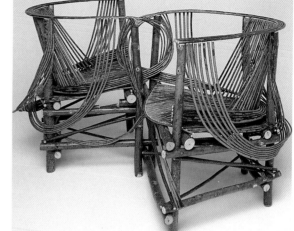

Right:
"Tête-a-Tête," Clifton
Montieth, MI

Left:
Bent willow chair,
Clifton Montieth, MI

Below:
Willow chair, rear view

Right:
Willow table, Clifton
Montieth, MI

Below:
Willow table, top view

Below right:
Painted willow grouping,
Monte Lindsley, WA

Upper left:
Antique bentwood rocker, Appalachians, c. 1900

Upper right:
Bent willow grouping, Michael Emmons, CA

Lower left:
Bent willow grouping, Monte Lindsley, WA

Lower right:
Bent willow chair, Paula Moody, Barry Jones, GA

RUSTIC TRADITIONS

Due to the wide availability of easily-bent willow wands and the simplicity of its construction, the classic bent-wood arm chair is probably the most commonly made and easily recognized item of rustic furniture. The design may be of Choctaw Indian or Gypsy origin, though some say it came from Africa. Bent willow furniture is frequently made by family groups, like these pieces made for three generations in North Carolina. See page 91.

Above:
Bent hazel chair, John Makepeace, England

Right:
Bent willow grouping, Odell family, NC

Upper left:
Bent willow chair,
Michael Emmons, CA

Upper right:
Bent willow group-
ing, Greg Adams, IN

Below:
Bent willow group-
ing, Paula Moody,
Barry Jones, GA

Below:
Bent willow chair,
Greg Adams, IN

Above:
Bent willow chair,
Elaine Shay, Liz Sifrit
Hunt, OH

Left:
Bent willow group-
ing, Greg Adams, IN

SPLIT WORK, MOSAIC, AND SWISS WORK

These are the various names for a style in which full or half-round branches are nailed or glued over a frame. This technique creates volume and intricacy, delicacy and geometry. It is careful, tedious work with often spectacular results. By using different woods or different forms of the same species, a rich visual variety can be achieved.

Right:
Mosaic topped table,
Greg Adams, IN

Below:
Detail of antique, mosaic
covered desk, courtesy
Robert Doyle

Right:
Star mosaic stand,
c. 1900, courtesy
Mary K. Darrah

Below left:
Antique mosaic dresser,
courtesy Mary K. Darrah

Below right:
Bent willow grouping
with mosaic table,
Monte Lindsley, WA

Right:
Mosaic trimmed
antique table, courtesy
Mary K. Darrah

Below:
Log-house box-top table
with removable roof,
Clifton Monteith, MI

Below right:
Willow inlaid table,
Greg Adams, IN

Upper left: Heart inlaid tables, Greg Adams, IN

Upper right: Antique mosaic desk, courtesy Robert Doyle

Lower left: Mosaic work on desk, Thomas Philips, NY

Lower right: Antique mosaic chair, c. 1920, MI

BARK WORK

Bark work is a technique in which birch or cedar bark is appliqued over a wooden frame. Often, the edges of the surface are finished with Swiss work. Rarely used on chairs, bark work is found most often on cupboards, tables, desks, blanket chests, clocks, picture frames, etc. It is most common in areas where durable bark from birch or cherry is readily available.

There are a number of talented bark-work makers in the Adirondack Mountains of New York. The Ojibwa Indians in the Bedjidi, Minnesota, area also produce a wide range of traditional and contemporary birch-bark designs.

Birch and cherry bark can be harvested twice a year from live, standing trees. With care, the tree is not damaged by this process, and will continue to produce bark for years.

Below:
Birch bark baskets,
Ojibwa Indians, MN,
courtesy Ladyslipper
Designs

Above:
Birch bark baskets, Ojibwa Indians, MN,
courtesy Ladyslipper Designs

Right:
Birch bark corner hutch, Barry Gregson, NY

Right:
Birch table with birch bark trim,
Jean Armstrong, NY

Below:
Birch covered Grandfather Clock,
courtesy Robert Doyle

Below right:
Birch sideboard, Ernest Stowe, c.
1900-11, Upper Saranac Lake, NY

Upper left:
Birch bark mirror frame, Jean
Armstrong, NY

Lower left:
Mirror frame, Ernest Stowe,
c. 1900, courtesy Robert Doyle

Harvesting Birch Bark, Tom Phillips, NY

THE DECORATIVE POSSIBILITIES OF BIRCH AND CEDAR BARK

(From an August 1911 article in Country Life in America by Benjamin G. Fernald)

The interior decoration of the rustic summer home or wilderness camp is a field where angels might well fear to tread, so easy is it to do the incongruous rather than the appropriate thing. Fortunately, the woods themselves offer—almost everywhere—simple and inexpensive materials for modifying and making harmonious the interior, as well as exterior, of the log cabin camp.

The easiest procured and most readily worked material is the bark of cedar trees and the various birches. Used singly or together, they can be made to harmonize or contrast perfectly, for both exterior and interior trimmings, with the logs of the cabin, whether the latter are covered with bark or peeled. Rough bark is used with unpeeled logs, and smooth bark with peeled logs. In the latter case, birch bark is used with the inside exposed.

Cedar bark does not lend itself to much modification, but a wide range of surfaces and colors is available in birch bark. Without any modification, and by using both sides of the bark and splitting it, the most picturesque color schemes can be evolved, ranging from a rich orange to pure whites and warm blacks, and from surfaces as smooth as paper to roughness of the shaggy sort.

For the exterior of the cabin, cedar bark is best adapted and most durable; all exposed planking can be covered with it to advantage, even the window and door frames.

Beautiful doors and cupboards can be fashioned from the cheapest of unplaned and even knotty boards when they are covered with birch and cedar bark. All partitions and ceilings can be wainscoted and paneled with the same materials.

Bark must be peeled in the spring or summer when the sap is running. For the purpose of decorating, rather large pieces of birch bark are required and it is best to fell the tree before barking it. Of course, the circumference of the tree determines the width of the piece of bark, but the length may vary from three to six feet.

The bark is first cut circumferentially at the proper intervals, by means of a saw or axe, clear through into the wood of the trunk. A longitudinal cut connecting the "girdle" cut is next made, and the bark removed, much as an orange is peeled. A dull axe blade or stick of wood several feet long, sharpened to a wedge end, is used to pry up the bark to start and aid in the peeling process, which is started at the longitudinal cut.

When first removed, the bark is curled up but pliable. It should immediately be spread flat and ten to twelve pieces clamped between scantlings held together at the ends by rope, wire, or strips of wood nailed on. This crate will hold the pieces flat while they season and dry out. The rough, shaggy part of the outer bark can be removed while the bark is dry by tearing it off with the hands.

For smooth peeling of the outer bark, it is necessary to steam the bark or soak it in water, subsequently drying it in crates as mentioned above. These crates permit the bark to shrink somewhat in seasoning without cracking, whereas if it is nailed in place while green or wet, it may crack afterward, particularly if a fire is maintained in the cabin for protracted periods.

As cedar trees are seldom large in diameter, the bark must necessarily be gathered in long strips rather than squares. There is some danger of splitting cedar bark in handling after it is dried, as it is slightly corrugated in structure. This is, however, of no importance, as the pieces can be placed so close together in nailing on the board backing that the joint is hidden by the fraying of the fibrous surface at the edges.

No special care in attaching either cedar or birch bark is necessary, other than to use nails of small diameter, such as wire shingle nails. For wainscoting and ceiling, large-headed nails of iron wrought in an ornamental design are effective.

I know of no more durable form of cellulose than birch bark, and have never seen a decayed piece. It lasts years after the entire trunk of the tree has decayed, and rings of it are found on the ground with no part of the trunk left. I do not believe cedar bark is as durable, but it will last as long as most unpainted, sawed lumber when exposed to the weather, or inside.

ROOT AND BURL WORK

Root and burl work involves using the earthy parts of trees—stumps, burls, or roots—to make furniture. The roots of mountain laurel or rhododendron are traditional favorites for this type of rustic building. It is particularly challenging work, calling for mole-like collecting, thorough washing, and then deft aesthetic and technical skills to combine the gangly roots into a properly-scaled piece of furniture. A successful piece is a breathtaking monument to things that grow in the earth.

Burls, those wart-like knobs you sometimes see on trunks and limbs, are natural growths formed by a tree to protect or heal itself from infections or irritations caused by insects. When cut off the tree, burls reveal a beautifully intricate grain pattern that is valued for use in veneers. Some rustic makers split the burl and polish the grain face for use as a table top. Others use the burled trunk or limb as a design element in stick or log furniture.

Below:
Burled canopy bed,
Brent McGregor, OR

Left: Burled table, Mike Patrick, WY

Right: Root chair, Don King, CO

Below: Root bed, maple, Daniel Mack, NY

Above left:
Root ball table, Tom Phillips, NY

Above right:
Burly root table, Philip Clausen, OR

Below: Philip Clausen, OR

Above left:
Burled bed, Mike Patrick, WY

Above right:
Burly root stand, Philip Clausen, OR

RUSTIC TRADITIONS

For the imaginative rustic maker, the strange globular shapes of tree burls are like rare pearls begging to become the focal points of monumental furniture creations. Few if any have used burls more effectively than Thomas Molesworth, the "rustic character" from Cody, Wyoming, who offered a bounty to cowboys for bringing him burled wood from their travels. He built this massive four-cushion sofa in 1933 for a wealthy rancher. See page 87.

Left:
Chair with burl seat/back, Barry Gregson, NY

RUSTIC VARIATIONS

There are people working with trees and other natural materials that are part of the rustic tradition and rustic spirit, but which do not fit neatly into "styles." Nonetheless, they belong in a discussion of contemporary rustic work.

WOVEN AND ENTWINED rustic furniture combines the bentwood approach with the basketmaker's craft. Thin branches or vines are more or less woven into a sturdy shape.

Right: Mirror and hall table, Paula Moody, Barry Jones, GA

Below: Entwined chair, ornamental tree cuttings, Margaret Craven, CO

Right: Entwined sideboard, Margaret Craven, CO

GRAIN LINE WORK uses the interior grain lines of the wood as a natural guide to form shapes for furniture. It is a variation of traditional country woodworking in which chairs are whacked out of logs by splitting and re-shaping the green wood. Instead of cutting the green wood into round posts and rungs, the furniture parts are shaped to reflect the way the grain of the log split out. I have made maybe a hundred chairs and table bases in this style.

Grain-split chairs and bar stools, Daniel Mack, NY

COLORED AND DYED WOODS: Rustic work doesn't have to exhibit a natural finish. However, the application of paints or dyes tends to create an entirely different, and often striking, visual impact. Some makers use muted tones to enhance the "antique" feel of a piece, while others apply bold colors to create a sleek, modern look.

Right:
Bent willow chaise longue, Monte Lindsley, WA

Below left:
Bentwood chair, colored, Barry Schwartz, Ny

Below right: Bentwood chair, colored, Barry Schwartz, NY

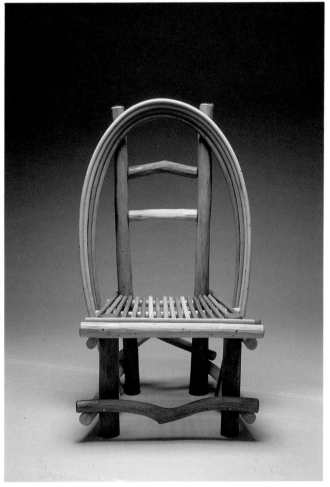

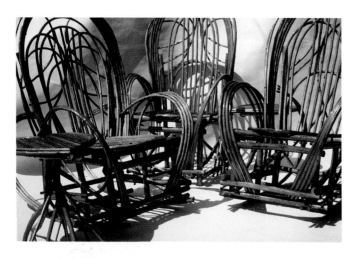

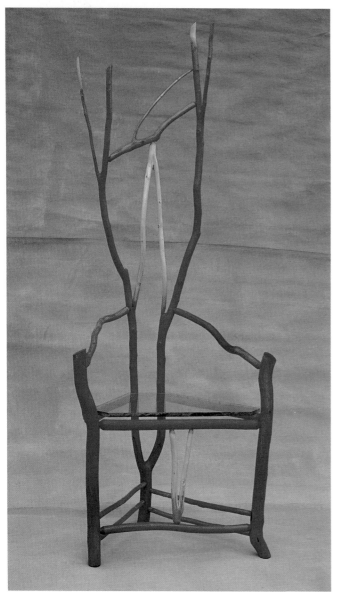

Above left:
Bent willow grouping, Monte Lindsley, WA

Above right:
Bent willow chair, Monte Lindsley, WA

Below left:
"Mercury" chair, serviceberry, color, Don King, CO

Below right:
Bent willow chair, Monte Lindsley, WA

DRIFTWOOD: This is an obvious choice of material for makers who live near oceans, lakes, or rivers, where the natural processes of decay and erosion help to "finish" the surface of the wood. Left long enough in such a hostile environment, even milled lumber begins to lose its hard edges, reverting toward its original form. Such found pieces have the added mystery of a former life: perhaps as part of a sunken ship or merely the bottom step of a seaside cottage.

Right: Bedside table, Catskill Mountain driftwood, Judd Weisberg, NY

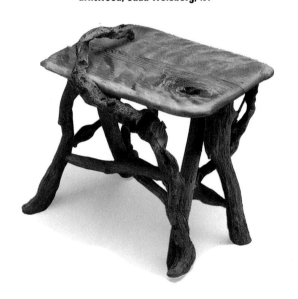

Right: End table, cherry, Catskill Mountain driftwood, Judd Weisberg, NY

Below: Coffee table, Catskill Mountain, driftwood, glass top, Judd Weisberg, NY

Top: Loveseat recliner, Catskill Mountain driftwood, Judd Weisberg, NY

Below left: Bench with back, San Francisco Bay driftwood, Susan Parish, CA

Below right: End table, San Francisco Bay Driftwood, Susan Parish, CA

MIXED MATERIALS such as metal, stone, old tools, and other organic elements—often antlers and horns—commonly find their way into work that, while not entirely natural, still can be called rustic.

Top left:
"Harp Chair," manzanita, cherry, willow, Don King, CO

Top right:
"Genesis," mixed woods, lexan, Don King, CO

Below:
Settee, maple, steerhide, Don King, CO

Far left:
Cherry chair with cherry pitter top, Daniel Mack, NY

Left:
"Tools in Motion," chairmaker's chair, Daniel Mack, NY

Below:
"Whisk Chair," maple, willow, deerskin, Don King, CO

Right:
"Kudu" chair, mixed
woods, steerhide,
Don King, CO

Far right:
Vanity, diamond
willow, Jake Lemon,
WY

Below:
Table, sandblasted
juniper base, Brent
McGregor, OR

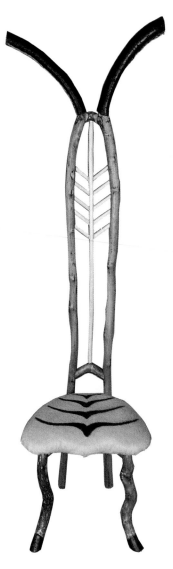

Top left:
"Rugbeater Chair," maple, woven seat, Daniel Mack, NY

Below left:
Settee, birch, stone, Don King, CO

Top right:
Moose antler chair with lilac frame, Jerry Farrell, NY

Below right:
Electrified dictionary stand, maple, auto paint, stirrup, Don Erdman, CO

Western rustic variations in the style of Thomas Molesworth, by Mike Patrick, WY

RUSTIC
TRADITIONS

Mixed materials were fundamental to the "ranch style" furniture of Thomas Molesworth. Ironwork, leather, Native American blankets, rope, horns, antlers, bones, hooves, skins, and even animal heads were incorporated into Molesworth's creations. He once used a creel as the central component of a magazine rack designed for the home of President Dwight D. Eisenhower, an avid fly fisherman. This antler-handle dresser was typical of the Molesworth style.

See page 87.

GROWN AND GRAFTED. If we think of rustic building as a synthesis of the maker's imagination and nature's whimsy, then perhaps the ultimate rustic statement was made by John Krubsack of Embarrass, Wisconsin, who—over a period of 11 years—literally "grew" a chair from living trees. Krubsack was a banker and farmer who had studied the art of plant grafting and who, in 1908, decided to test his skill with an unusual project.

Krubsack planted 28 box elder seeds in a carefully-designed pattern. After a few years, he began to train the direction of the saplings' growth along a trellis, and eventually grafted the trees together at critical points to form the arms, seat, and back of the chair. At the end of ten years, Krubsack cut all the trees except the legs, which he allowed to strengthen for an additional year. Dubbed "The Chair That Grew," Krubsack's creation became a popular curiosity in the 1920s. It toured the country with several exhibitions and was featured in *Ripley's Believe It Or Not*.

**Right:
John Krubsack
seated in trained
and grafted trees.**

**Far right:
John Krubsack
seated in his
finished chair.**

STORIES ABOUT TREE-CROSSED PEOPLE

There is, of course, another side to the rustic equation. Beyond the region, the trees, the styles, and the influences, are the motivations—those murky drives that keep people fiddling and tweaking with sticks for hours on end. Depending on the eye, the skills, and the imagination of the maker, the result can be a beautiful forest sculpture or perhaps no more than a pile of misshapen sticks. This chapter is a collection of stories about people making rustic furniture.

Rustic makers come from all walks of life. They are driven from all walks of life. Some try to make rustic work a new vocation. Some succeed. Others keep rustic work as a complement to more mainstream engagements. Then there are the eccentrics, the makers who have been somehow transformed by their rustic experience. They share a passion that sets their creations apart from other rustic work.

Eccentric rustic is unabashed in its use of color and texture; its attempts at humor, satire, sentimentality, and other human emotions. Eccentric work often combines diverse materials with natural forms. It's as if the child-poet-creator was set loose in the woods and these chairs, settees, beds, and tables are the result of an afternoon's hard play with the trees.

Looking at eccentric rustic, it's not always easy to separate the tree from the person who transformed it. There is an animation, a grace, a meld of human-tree characteristics that can be disorienting to all but the knowing (and eccentric) buyer. Throughout the history of rustic furniture, there have always been the eccentric makers. With a little research, I have found several personal stories about the magnetic draw of rustic furniture making.

In this one, from a design book published in 1883, the unnamed author describes his vacations spent making rustic furniture:

"**W**hen I go to my place in the summer, it is after nine months hard work in my profession and I want rest from continual reading, writing, and thinking. I can't spend all my time in riding and rowing. Hunting, fishing, and farming have no attractions for me, and so as a last resort, I have fallen into the habit of tinkering as a carpenter.

The abundance of 'crooked sticks' all around me soon gave my labor the direction of rustic work, so that now I have three summer houses, five or six seats, large and small, under the shade of the tree, several arbors, and quite a number of chairs and sofas scattered about the place—all of rustic work—and every year I add something to the list. The work interests me and pleasantly fills up my vacations.

All the work is made very strong and substantial, and is put together with nails of different sizes, and perhaps an occasional screw. The only implements used are a hammer, a saw, a hatchet, and a gimlet, with abundance of strong twine to bind the pieces together to see how they will answer. Sometimes one favorite crooked stick will be tried half a dozen ways to see where it will look best, and sometimes half a dozen different pieces will be tied (temporarily) in one place to see how best to fill it. When the decision is made, then comes the nailing, and when the pieces are firmly secured the strings are discarded.

The collection of the stuff in the first place is the great thing. It is only in a rocky country like the banks of Lake George (in upstate New York) that the stuff can be found in perfection. In the 'struggle for life' the roots and trunks and even the limbs of the trees have to turn and twine themselves in all directions, and thus is produced a variety of 'twistifications' that a level country and stoneless soil would not afford.

Two kinds of running vines, which grow in great abundance in that region, are of great service: the wild grape and the bitter-sweet. I have found the latter sometimes as large as four or five inches in diameter. Besides the natural twists of these vines, they can be interwoven and twisted into almost any shape when green.

The bark of the white birch and the hemlock I often use for ornamentation, as also the knobs or warts that grow on the chestnut. The trees are perfectly hardy so that we use any kind of wood that has a proper crook in it. These crooks assume such fantastic forms that almost all shapes can be found with little attention.

The seats of the outdoor sofas are made of maple saplings, all of about the same size and growing very straight. The tops of the table and of the sofa on the piazza are made of boards covered with strips of osier, alder, and maple, interwoven into any shape that fancy may choose. The nailing is all done with brads, finishing, and cut nails—tacks and wrought nails being avoided because of their heads, which are in the way, and of their tendency to make the stuff split.

The seats in my summer houses are either large flat stones, or pieces of squared logs, or long seats of maple saplings, or rustic chairs. One of the picturesque of those chairs was made from the contorted and gnarled limbs of a very ancient apple tree."

Another magazine article written in 1909 by David S. George relates his aesthetic approach to rustic furniture making. His observations seem as timely now as they were then:

"**M**y idea of an artistic piece of rustic furniture is one so constructed that it appears as if it might have grown from the soil; one in which every piece of wood starts somewhere, goes somewhere, and does something. There should be no useless sticks put in merely to fill up spaces. The main lines of a piece of furniture should be of the heaviest branches, the secondary parts of smaller pieces branching, apparently at least, from these.

The construction of a chair or settee so that it will be strong and comfortable in both seat and back requires no little patience and careful study. Aside from the general form desired, little can be planned out ahead. The chair must grow, pieces being selected to meet special requirements as the work progresses. Often a branch will suggest a particular part of a chair, as a foot or an arm. Sometimes it is possible to find two branches that are similar, as in the arms of the chair, where balance without symmetry was secured.

The main joints are made with brace and bit, fitting the end of one stick to the hole in another and nailing the joint fast. Sometimes one piece may be shaped to fit the surface of another, a knot or branch sustaining the weight.

A keyhole saw will be found very useful in fitting, and a bradawl is indispensable for starting the nails. I used finishing nails almost exclusively, dipping the nails in oil before using and driving with a light hammer to prevent bending the nails. The nails should be set in out of sight. If, whenever two pieces of wood cross, they are firmly nailed, a great deal will be added to the strength of the chair.

Generally speaking chairs should be made with but three legs, both on account of the difficulty in bringing four feet into the same plane and because most rustic chairs are used on the ground, where a chair with three legs will always stand better.

An interesting feature of this sort of rustic work is that each chair or table is individual. It is practically impossible to make two pieces alike."

At about this time—from the 1880s through the 1920s—there was a rustic boom. The rustic motif of New York City's Central Park and Brooklyn's Prospect Park had started a trend. The great camps of the Adirondacks were being built and furnished in grand rustic splendor. There, and in the Great Smoky Mountains, the Shenandoahs, the Catskills, and the Rockies, mountain hotels and spas became attractive, exotic getaways promising rejuvenation for the weary city folk as they sat in rustic rockers and ate from rustic tables.

The popularity of the great camps and other rustic retreats brought new opportunities for people struggling to make a living in those remote locales. Craig Gilborn, director of the Adirondack Museum in Blue Mountain Lake, New York, has done extensive research on the rustic builders of the great camp era, including Ernest Stowe, the bark master. Gilborn wrote about Stowe for *The Magazine Antiques:*

"The forests and lakes of the Adirondack Mountains have shaped a life of logging and outdoor sport in that section of northern New York State. In the late nineteenth and early twentieth centuries, a man's livelihood in the Adirondacks generally meant logging and working as a guide for small parties of city people who wanted a taste of the wild—and of the trout and venison found there.

Carpentry was another source of cash, although building resort hotels and summer cottages, like logging, often entailed weeks of absence from one's family. One variety of carpentry, so-called rustic work, was a sideline for men who had a talent for using some recognizable part of the tree to decorate a building. Rustic furniture was a further specialization in which a minority of rustic workers were engaged. For some, making rustic furniture was as much a way of keeping busy as it was of making money.

What little I know about Ernest Stowe was told me by Clarence and the late William Petty, brothers who were raised on Upper Saranac Lake and remembered Stowe from their childhood. Clarence Petty recalls that Stowe, a bachelor, was reticent man whose mouth seemed always ready to smile. He thinks Stowe came from Colton, New York, about sixty miles north of where he settled on Upper Saranac Lake.

According to Clarence, Stowe joined the teams of artisans and laborers building the 'camps,' or summer estates, of wealthy New Yorkers who were discovering the joys of the Adirondacks. In addition, he made furniture in the cabin he owned on land that belonged to Rustic Lodge, a hotel overlooking Upper Saranac Lake.

There he worked like a beaver, probably during the long winters, making furniture, which he stored in vacant buildings on hotel property and in a barn nearby. This industriousness surely explains why Stowe's output was larger than that of most other rustic furniture makers in the Adirondacks. I know of between fifty and sixty pieces of furniture attributable to Stowe, including three sets of dining chairs.

Stowe's furniture clearly shows that he was influenced by cabinetwork from outside the Adirondacks. The Secretary shown here, for instance, displays the attenuated proportions of Hepplewhite or Sheraton furniture, while details such as spandrels, quarter columns, cornices, and shaped skirts reveal a certain familiarity with the appearance of eighteenth-century furniture.

Birch sideboard, c. 1900–11, Ernest Stowe, NY

**Above:
Clarence Nichols
seated in his
first rocker.**

**Below:
Dining table
and six chairs,
1933–47,
Clarence
Nichols, NY**

Like other rustic furniture makers I have seen, Stowe used nails, not the dovetails of a cabinetmaker, yet he clothed his pieces in rustic materials in a manner unique in my experience. He always laid the white birch bark flat, with the seams straight and discernible only when seen up close, and the yellow birch rods, halved and shaped at their ends with a knife, are lined up like soldiers on review. However, Stowe's greatest triumph, it seems to me, is to have successfully juxtaposed stylish forms with rustic materials."

The story of another driven hobbyist-maker has recently become known. Clarence Nichols was neither a logger, a woodsman, nor a carpenter, but rather he was a baker in New York City. When sugar rationing was imposed in 1922, Nichols was forced out of business and moved his family upstate, where further misfortune led him into rustic work. In 1988, thirty-two pieces of his unique and stunningly beautiful furniture were exhibited by the New York State Museum in Albany, owners of the collection. In the catalogue, titled *The Rustic Artistry of Clarence O. Nichols,* Associate Curator of History John Scherer wrote about Nichols and the years following a 1924 fire that destroyed his home:

"**N**ecessity was the spur that forced Clarence to be both practical and creative at the same time. When the Nichols' farm house and its furniture burned, it was discovered that the renewal

Clockwise from top left: Armchair, 1932; hall chair, 1944; rocking chair, 1926; "Jack and Jill Chair," 1926; Clarence Nichols, NY

date for the insurance policy had passed and the family could retrieve nothing from its loss.

Thus it was that Nichols constructed the first of two houses with cedar posts, beams and trim. Stripped of bark, the cedar retained its twisted trunks and branch stubs; a large fireplace of granite dominated the living room, which in every other respect was snug and small in scale. This home was completed in 1926 and a second cottage, somewhat larger but with similar rustic detailing and a stone fireplace, was built close by in about 1930. The Nichols' family moved into this house and rented the other to tenants.

The Depression years were difficult ones for the family. Nichols earned money by doing carpentry work, while Mrs. Nichols commuted to New York City, where she worked as a lamp-shade designer for a decorator. Additional income was derived from renting the adjacent cottage.

Needing furniture for his home, Nichols turned to red cedars, which grew in the vicinity for material with which to build. He was drawn to cedar, his daughter said, when he was cutting firewood and noticed how beautiful the wood looked. He began building furniture in an organic or rustic style and developed a technique for handling the cedar.

His success lay in the process. He used the trunk and limbs of cedar trees for legs, table tops, and braces. He discovered that newly-cut cedar did not have a mellow appearance but dead cedar, easily found in the woods, had matured slowly and acquired a close, rich grain or figure. In addition it yielded a wine-red color (this is the same cedar from which 'hope chests' were fashioned two generations ago) and took on a satiny patina.

Nichols soon learned that he could make furniture that was both comfortable for sitting and interesting to see by splitting tree limbs lengthwise down the center and laying out the resultant pair side by side so that one half was the mirror image of the other. These he would assemble with long screws secured with a washer and nut in the rear. The furniture is sturdy and shows no evidence of having been nailed.

After removing the bark, Nichols scraped the cambium layer just underneath with the edge of a broken piece of glass and then sandpapered the surface until it was smooth. He successively varnished and sanded until the wood fairly glowed and gleamed, a delight to the eye and the hand.

Nichols hunted for cedars with interesting shapes and limbs. Similarity was difficult since no two trees were alike. It took him fourteen years to find material from which the backs of the dining chairs (see page 84) were fashioned.

Nichols completed his first piece of furniture, the rocking chair, in 1926. He continued to build and repair his cedar furniture, and created small items from this wood until his death in October, 1950.

Nichols furniture is evocative of nature harnessed to human needs, and it works on both levels—of artistry and function."

Not all rustic characters hail from the Northeast. As the railroads pushed westward, new settlers arrived on the frontier with few belongings and less in the way of furniture. Necessity, isolation, strange new influences, and previously unknown woods combined to create a rustic style that was truly western. In 1989, the Buffalo Bill Historical Center in Cody, Wyoming, organized an exhibition commemorating Thomas Molesworth, the premier stylemaker of western rustic. As curator Paul Fees wrote in the exhibit catalogue:

"**A**n unmistakable western style in furnishing was slow to develop, at least in part because most settlers in the frontier West hoped to recreate the comforts they had left behind. By the turn of the century, a Wyoming ranch house was likely to be furnished with mission oak furniture. It was sturdy and stylish and available by catalogue from Montgomery Ward or Sears and Roebuck.

Many homes had one or two antler chairs, mostly as novelties. Verandas and hunting camps might feature twig or rough pine furniture made locally. But the birth of a true western style awaited a catalyst, who arrived in the form of Thomas Canada Molesworth.

Molesworth was a manufacturer of 'homemade' furniture in Cody, Wyoming, when Pennsylvania publishing magnate Moses Annenberg commissioned him in 1933 to furnish the vast rustic retreat

The Grand Hotel, Billings, MT, c. 1955, lobby decorated and furnished by Thomas Molesworth. Courtesy Buffalo Bill Historical Center, Cody, WY.

**Above:
Thomas
Molesworth,
c. 1939**

**Below:
Burl chair,
Thomas
Molesworth,
photos courtesy
Buffalo Bill
Historical Center,
Cody, WY**

Annenberg built for himself in a remote corner of the 'Cowboy State.' In hiring Molesworth, Annenberg was following the tycoons of New York, who began in the 1870s to build homes and hunting lodges in the Adirondack Mountains. To emphasize and enhance their escape from the city, they furnished their retreats with the rustic creations of local craftsmen.

The Cody country had ties to rustic Adirondack tradition, ties of which Molesworth was aware. One of the dominant pieces of regional architecture was (and is) Pahaska Tepee, a rough but elegant log structure near the east entrance to Yellowstone National Park. Completed in 1905, Pahaska Tepee had been designed for Buffalo Bill Cody by A.A. Anderson, a classically trained artist and the scion of a wealthy New York family. Anderson was inspired by the great hunting lodges he had known in upstate New York.

Molesworth's response for Annenberg's 'Ranch A,' was to combine several traditional rustic and western elements in new and sophisticated ways. He made chairs and couches on massive pole frames with prominent pine burls and cushions of leather faced with contemporary fabrics. He created an almost 'Western Gothic' dining room with carved high-back chairs and a table for twenty, covered with leather, smoothly finished, and dyed white. Beds are carved with standing animal figures. End tables are of twig. Drapes are pale horsehide edged with beadwork.

The design and craftsmanship were heavy-handed and even

crude by Molesworth's later standards. But a style was born. By successfully uniting elements of the Southwest, mountains and plains, he had surpassed the localism of most rustic furniture makers.

Molesworth was, in fact, a trained and self-conscious artist. He was born in Kansas in 1890 to a prosperous preacher who moved his family to southeastern Montana, near Billings. He became an excellent horseman and an admirer of western art. Deciding to be a painter, he went east to the Art Institute of Chicago. There he excelled in his studio work, despite living his life as artistically as a generous allowance permitted.

**Above left:
Dresser with antler drawer pulls,
Thomas Molesworth**

**Above right:
Single bed with carved deer silhouette, c. 1933,
Thomas Molesworth**

**Left:
Reading room of Kalif Temple, Sheridan, WY, designed and furnished by Thomas Molesworth.
Photos courtesy Buffalo Bill Historical Center, Cody, WY**

The Art Institute was a leading force in the world of modern decorative arts. Molesworth also was immersed in the Arts and Crafts Movement, which began in the 1880s as a response to the machine age and the attendant loss of craftsmanship in manufacturing.

Molesworth labored for a time for a Chicago furniture firm and later managed the Rowe Furniture Co. in Billings, Montana. In 1931, married and with two small children, Molesworth decided that he would 'rather die broke than work for someone else,' and moved his family south to Cody, where he opened his own furniture business.

The Annenberg commission launched his career as a designer and manufacturer. It was not long before his work was much in demand for hotel lobbies—including the Stockmen's Hotel in Elko, Nevada, the Wort in Jackson, Wyoming, the Northern in Billings, and Cheyenne's famed Plains Hotel—for dude ranches, guest lodges, and for other public spaces. For a while, his furniture was marketed to wealthy sportsmen worldwide by Abercrombie and Fitch.

Molesworth's creations inspired many imitators, some of them innovative craftsmen of the 'ranch style' of furniture. His own pieces are gradually disappearing from public view—away from the hotels and lodges he decorated, and into the homes of appreciative collectors. Sturdily built of top-grade materials, they will last for generations.

Just as the rustic is supposed to evoke country and nature, Molesworth's work evokes the West. The effect is far more complex than a simple mediation between urban and rural or between the drawing room and the hunting lodge. Like the paintings of the best western artist, the furniture and roomscapes allow their audience to appreciate—without embarrassment—the West of romance."

**Right:
A grouping of southern willow furniture designed by Odell and built today by his son and grandsons.**

The South also has its rustic characters. Since the mid 1970s, Barbara Plott, owner of Added Oomph!, a furniture business in High Point, N.C., has been selling bent willow furniture that has been made in North Carolina by the same family for three generations:

"I first met Odell in 1973. I saw some bent willow twig furniture at a gas station and asked about it. I was sent down the road. There was Odell. He was around 70 years of age, drank a little, and made willow furniture the same way he'd been making it since the Depression.

I'll always remember his story. During the thirties, he had no money and a woman came to him with a picture of a twig chair and asked if he could make one similar. He gathered the swamp willow and produced 'the funniest looking chair I ever did see.' For this he was paid five dollars and discovered a way to make money that was going to carry him and his family through many years.

With the first five dollars and some additional cash, he bought a wagon and hitched his horse and sold twig furniture within a fifty-mile radius of home. As the cash came in, he soon was able to buy a pickup truck and hired three men to work with him. He even produced chairs for Hollywood. Occasionally I've seen Odell's work on the front porches of log cabins in the late-show movies of the thirties and forties.

Sometime during the late forties, the work slacked off and Odell went back to making the furniture for friends and neighbors. By the time I met the family, his son Frank and two grandsons were working with him. They felt very strongly about keeping the willow furniture production within the family. Even though his son did auto body work in the front yard and willow furniture in the side yard, they felt that while other businesses came and went, they could always make money with the twig, no matter how hard the times.

The furniture has always been made the same. They go into the swamps anywhere from Virginia to as far south as Georgia— swishing the branches to keep the snakes from biting—and cut the young willow trees for bending and the heavier ones for framework. No steaming or power tools were ever used. They used the fresh pieces within two or three days for bending and the only tools were hammers and saws. Odell only had a second-grade education, but an innate sense of design and construction.

My company, Added Oomph!, began selling twig furniture around 1975. At that time Odell had two styles of chairs and settees: 'Fan-Back' and 'Old

Bent willow canopy bed, Odell family, NC

Odell's son Frank and his son Henry

Fashion,' and he would make any size coffee table or end table. I expanded the line to include a bed, a chaise lounge, a dining table, etc. Odell, Frank and I would work out design and proportions, in the side yard, on the back of the Winn Dixie (grocery) store bag. We never veered very far from their original design.

Odell died several years ago, but his son Frank and Frank's sons continue to make this beautiful furniture."

This more or less gets us into the second half of the twentieth century, a moment of eclipse for the rustic. Mid-century design had little use for the rustic. Aluminum, plastic, and plywood were the materials of the period, not barky wood.

It was the "baby-boomers" who rediscovered rustic. Attracted by the same simple, natural magnetism that had drawn various social and philosophical movements a hundred years before, the rustic look appealed to the corporate burnouts, the naturalists, and the members of the growing "back to the land" movement.

Rustic had the romance, the air of self-sufficiency, the no-overhead look, and the natural spiritualism, later recognized as "low tech, high touch." The graceful simplicity of a rustic chair was appropriate for those experimenting with meditation, stress reduction, and Zen. This increasing popularity was enhanced by a growing appetite for things that fit into the "country look," then the "Santa Fe look," then "the eclectic room."

The rustic makers of today are seen as folk artists, neo-barbarians, and outsiders. But trees are trees and the designs of today echo those of years ago. Likewise, people are people and contemporary stories of lives redirected by the lure of rustic building seem oddly familiar. Greg Adams is one of many modern rustic characters who discovered a new creative outlet in the woods:

"From my early childhood, I was around the lumber business, and as the old circus adage goes, sawdust really does get into your blood. The smells of sawdust and varnish and the sounds of saws and hammers can put me back there instantly.

I can remember fishing scraps out of the mill scrap box and nailing them together when I went to my grandpa's lumberyard on Saturday or after school. I made ships and airplanes. I learned how to nail when I was five or six. But I never did learn to be a good carpenter. I flunked the first six weeks of shop class—the only 'F' I ever got. I was always intimidated by the prospect of making anything from finished lumber.

One day, years later, while fishing on the banks of the Wabash River, I started toying with the willow saplings growing next to me. The fish weren't biting and I was attracted to the color, flexibility, and texture of the willow. I had some clippers with me and I cut off a pile and took them home with me and just jumped in, trying to make a basket. I soon learned that trying to find a workable technique would take lots of trial and error and went to the library to get some books on baskets.

After that, I couldn't stop. For three years, I made baskets and started showing and selling them at local shows. At one craft festival I ran into a fellow who had made willow furniture. I was impressed. He told me he was going to get out of willow because he was having trouble finding a good supply. I knew where there were abundant supplies of the larger saplings needed and decided to try—despite my intimidation with carpentry. My first effort, made in 1984, is still around. Fairly flimsy, poorly proportioned, flawed: it still convinced me I could do this.

Five years later, with 100 craft shows, folk art shows, fine art shows, and festivals behind me, I am getting better all the time and I learn something every day.

The furniture I make is in keeping with my personality. Approximate and non-symetrical suits me better. I nail pieces together and then cut off the excess. While I am envious of the joinery technique of some other rustic furniture makers, it is just not in me. I guess what attracts me the most about what I do is the complete absence of concern for uniformity or precision. I do try to make my items sturdy, level and comfortable, but I just get there differently. I strive for balance, not regularity.

Furniture making is a direct and concrete alternative to the amorphous and intangible work I do as a child welfare caseworker with abused and neglected children and their families. My job is a constant barrage of hostility, frustration, and meaninglessness. But each time I put the final touch on my latest chair, table, or stand, I still get the same feeling of directness and accomplishment. For me, this has been a balancing force in my life. I don't think I could have stayed with my job as long as I have without it."

Greg Adams making a willow chair at his home in Muncie, IN.

An encounter with rustic furniture can be both mysterious and profound, lingering in the subconscious and exerting an influence long after details of the memory have faded. Photographer, sculptor, and blacksmith Bobby Hansson has been building rustic, "neo-viking" chairs for many years. While shooting photographs for this book, Hansson discovered that, in addition to his romantic connection

with seafaring ancestors, his furniture style has had another, deeper, yet previously unrealized source of inspiration:

"**W**hen my mother-in-law gave me Craig Gilborn's *Adirondack Furniture* for Christmas, I was so delighted that I agreed to write a review of it for *American Craft Magazine*. I began with this true story:

'Just like sitting in a tree,' thought the boy, as his legs dangled from the bark-covered throne. He ran his hand over the arm made of gnarled roots. It was cleanly sliced, thickly varnished, and smoother than glass.

'Like sitting in a tree...but better.' It was made of yellow birch, high, deep, and very sturdy. Paul Bunyan himself couldn't have had a better chair. There were knobby parts, twiggy parts, and sections that were perfect for climbing.

'The chair was in Worden Camp in the Adirondacks. The year was 1943. I had never sat in anything so wonderful.'

In 1990, two years after I wrote this, Dan Mack and I were driving through the Adirondacks, headed toward Lake Placid, when I saw a sign for Schroon Lake. I told Dan the story of the chair and we decided to see if we could find it.

Bobby Hansson in his rural Maryland workshop

I telephoned Winifred Sherburne, Frank Worden's niece, and was dismayed to hear that, like so many of the old camps, Pine Point, the cottage with the chair, is only a memory now. It had been sold to strangers, demolished, and replaced by a modern home.

'There was a rustic chair,' I said to her. 'Do you remember?'

'Oh, yes!' she replied. 'Charles Worden made that while he was building the camps in 1915. We've got it. We keep it in the boat-house.' She paused, then added, 'Would you like to come over and see it?'

An hour later, Dan and I were led through the trees, over moss-covered rocks, to the edge of the lake, and to the boathouse. Brushing aside cobwebs, Wini unlocked the door and we climbed the narrow stairs. There in the darkness we found the chair.

We brought it out into the sunlight. It was a little like seeing your very first girlfriend after forty years. I stood there, staring, lost in a swirl of memories. Then I noticed that Dan, who was standing near-by, had begun to chuckle, then to laugh out loud.

'That's YOUR chair!' he said, grinning. 'That's the chair you've been building!'

Stick chair, Charles Worden, c. 1915, Schroon Lake, NY

I looked again. He was right. The resemblance to my 'style' was undeniable. The right arm was made from a strange, forked piece with a root knob on the end. Seventy-five years earlier, Charles Worden had found that odd stick and built this chair around it: not quite symmetrical, each joint a different style, yet related; sturdy, yet with a feeling of movement. Thirty years later, I discovered that I had learned all that, without realizing it, from this chair.

What else had I absorbed during those summers in the woods? I remembered 'Uncle Frank' Worden and his workshop in the boathouse, where I would gaze wistfully at the vast array of tools: the razor-sharp planes and chisels, the huge, two-man saws, the murderous looking double-edged axes, peaveys, augers, rasps, and an enormous Stillson wrench, its jaws as big as a bear's.

Like the spirit of the chair, that love of old tools has stayed with me. I have lots of them. Some handed down from my father. Some from Jose' de Creeft, who taught me stone carving and black-smithing. Others I collected at auctions and yard sales. I learn from them all. Some provide examples of what to strive for when I make my own tools. But more importantly, they bind me to the past and give me a feeling of continuity with these craftsmen. It's as if these tools of men long-dead guide my hand, just as my hand guides the tools.

Sometimes I can even hear my father's voice: a little loud, a trifle impatient saying, 'Don't force it. Let the saw do the work...'

Dan's voice broke my reverie. 'We have to get some photos of this for the book,' he said.

As I began to focus the camera, I noticed that something seemed different. I remembered that as a child, sitting in this chair, I had felt surrounded; engulfed in its huge, wooden arms. Now I could barely squeeze into it (probably because I weigh four or five times what I weighed then). I remembered feeling totally safe in that chair. Now I was afraid I would bust it in two.

'Are you sure there isn't another chair, sort of like this one, but different?' I asked the Sherburnes hopefully.

'No,' they said. 'Just this one.'

I've been taking photographs for many years. I've made my living capturing images through lenses—for films, for television, for magazines, and for books. I've shot hundreds of chair photographs. Yet for some reason, when I photographed this chair, without thinking, I positioned it—like a novice—in some tall grass, where it blended in with the background. It almost disappeared.

It was as if, unconsciously, I didn't want Dan to have a photo of

**Left:
Stick chair,
Bobby
Hansson, MD**

**Right:
"Neo-Viking
Throne,"
Bobby
Hansson, MD**

this chair. I wanted him to have a photo that would show him the way sitting in that chair had made me feel, way back before he was even born. The power that an object can have cannot be shown in a photo, or described in words. So I guess that's why I build chairs.

Each chair I make is different. But now I see that each one, in its own way, is an attempt to capture a bit of the magic I got from the Worden chair. Any time I can find a glimpse, just a taste of it, I am inspired to try again. I think that—since I'm aiming for that impossible chair—production, efficiency, even selling isn't that important to me. I find myself working more like a sculptor than a furniture maker.

Five years ago, I built nothing but what I called 'Neo-Viking Thrones.' They were massive and rough, as if built for some mythic race of Nordic warriors. I worked directly with the wood, without drawings or plans, and used only old hand tools, or tools I had forged myself, as if that self-sufficiency would make the throne even more an expression of my ideas and feelings.

I've been making chairs for decades, but it has only been since I saw that Worden chair again that I realized the extent to which I am trying to recapture the way that chair affected me. Moving from the city to the country changed my choice of materials and brought me closer to nature. Seeing that chair brought the underlying motivations into sharper focus.

I loved that chair. I loved the way I felt in it: secure, powerful, safe. I try to capture that feeling when I build today, that sense of monumentality. I want my chairs to lend power, as well as protection, to anyone sitting in them.

Like a throne, I guess."

THE RUSTIC PAST: ONE MAKER'S
TWISTED VERSION OF THE HISTORY OF RUSTIC FURNITURE

There is no easily-charted, linear evolution to the history of rustic furniture; no scholarly chronology of design innovation and cross-cultural influence. Rather it begins in hundreds of small, personal streams of memory and experience that join to create a larger, longer public record: The cool shade of a tree on a hot day. The hypnotic waving of leaves and branches. The seemingly endless secrecy of gnarly bark. The ancient, pleasant, fearful smell of decaying leaves. The crisp snapping of dead twigs. The cavities in trees—homes for birds, squirrels, gnomes.

I remember the woods behind the house of my childhood, full of larch trees, forever green and soft with needles. Beneath the lowest branches there was a space, a room. It had a carpet of needles surrounding the big trunk, and that place was a hidden place. To be there was to have both a scared and calm feeling all at once. The smell was different, the feel, the temperature, the humidity.

That place was quite near my home, yet so alien and so attractive. Just beyond the larches were some alders, or maybe they were soft maples: trees to climb, to build tree houses, and to make bows and arrows from the straight young shoots. There, in that earthy home beneath the larches, a certain personal and collective history of rustic furniture begins.

Today, forty years later, my three daughters repeat this proto-

history beneath the cherry tree and forsythia bushes behind the barn. They hide themselves off, inhale the muskiness of the earth beneath, and exhale a series of stories about how it is they came to live here, the tragedies and challenges that make up their make-believe moments. People who like, or make, or buy rustic furniture are in touch with this part of our history.

In the Orient there is an independent tradition of the rustic style that may date back as much as a thousand years. One of the oldest existing depictions of rustic furniture is a thirteenth-century copy of a tenth-century painting that shows a Chinese scholar seated in a gnarled stick chair. The Western tradition goes back at least to the eighteenth century and probably has its inspiration in earlier Gothic times. Indeed the gothic arch itself can be seen as just a formal architectural rendering of the arching branches of a tree.

As a reaction against the strict formality of Victorian style, it became common among landscape designers and architects to make use of rustic elements to introduce elements of frivolity into formal, traditional gardens. These were places of disorganization and mystery in the otherwise controlled plan, a deviation from order that was seen as a needed relief. These included the grotto, or underground cave, and the "folly," the useless amusement in the corner of the garden. These were commonly rustic structures or just newly-constructed "ruins." Nonetheless, for the garden visitor, they were a momentary pleasure to stumble upon. There was also the hermitage, the abode of the hermit. Some of these had a rustic, ascetic quality.

The rustic spirit came to America from Europe in the mid nineteenth century largely due to the influence of Andrew Jackson Downing, America's foremost landscape designer at the time. He advocated rustic work as the ideal furnishing for outdoor settings and made liberal use of stick lattice work, log bridges, rustic buildings, and especially log seats in his landscape designs. As he noted in an 1841 treatise on landscaping theory, "There is scarcely a prettier or more pleasant object for the termination of a long walk in the pleasure-grounds or park, than a neatly thatched structure of rustic work, with its seat for repose and a view of the landscape beyond."

Downing inspired the architects Calvert Vaux and Frederick Law Olmsted, who created many great public parks, notably Central Park in Manhattan and Prospect Park in Brooklyn. In both these parks the rustic idiom is prominent and was novel in its day. Like other park visitors, the wealthy industrialists living nearby were amused and inspired by rustic designs. William West Durant, J. Pierpont Morgan, Alfred G. Vanderbilt, and others carried these the ideas with them to create their own private rustic worlds at their great summer homes, or "camps," in the Adirondack Mountains of northern New York State. (Yes, the "Adirondack look" came from Europe via New York City to the mountains!)

But at the same time the effects of industrialization continued to puzzle America. There were exploding urban populations and their attendant problems: immigrants, more immigrants, machines, devices, and useless inventions. The draw of the rustic, the bucolic, seemed like a bosom of quiet comfort in a world of discord. Medically and spiritually, nature and contact with nature was believed to have restorative powers. Vacations and even country homes were seen to be an important part of a healthy life.

Country Life in America, a magazine published at the turn of the century (that sounds remarkably contemporary today), instructed people on the many ways for urban dwellers to keep in touch with "the coun-

try." Rustic furniture, indeed the regenerative powers of building rustic furniture, were often written about. People came to see rustic furniture as their own little bit of nature. It was a cheap, transportable memory of a vacation or another place and time. It still is.

Enterprising Scots and Irish, living in the Appalachian Mountains, began building fanciful rockers and other rustic pieces to sell to tourists. Rural families, mostly in the South, would clip their weed patches of willow and create inexpensive, quickly-built backyard furniture. In the Midwest, entire farms were established to grow straight young hickory trees for mass-produced, commercial rustic furniture. Known as "Old Hickory Furniture," it is still grown and built today.

As the railroad pushed west, bringing money and homesteaders from the east, the settlers took along the custom of associating the "rustic look" with status. In fact much of the "Western" aesthetic can be seen as overgrown "Eastern rustic." At various times Native Americans, including the Mic Mac of Maine, the Onondaga of western New York,

Bottom left:
Summerhouse at Richmond Hill, Asheville, NC, c. 1893.

Bottom right:
Thomas Edison seated in a rustic chair, c. 1917.

and the Seminoles of Florida, have produced forms of rustic "tourist" furniture. In the Northeast, little bits of balsam, pine, and birch were commonly made into souvenir frames, pillows, and accessories easily carried back to the cities.

For twenty good years around the turn of the century, talented (and even untalented) carpenters in the Adirondack Mountains found they could make part of a living concocting fanciful furniture—chairs, tables, beds, settees—for the "camps" of wealthy summer residents. They included trees, limbs, roots, bark, and even incorporated leather, horns, hooves, bones, taxidermy, and forged metal into their designs.

But changing income tax laws put an end to the explosion of the great camps. Money wasn't as free as it had been and the indulgences of the great camps became less popular. The harsh realities brought by two World Wars made the fantasy "life beneath the trees" a harder one to embrace. The market for rustic work declined for nearly fifty years. Newly developed plastics, aluminum alloys, and other spin-offs of war production replaced wood (and particularly trees) for use in furniture. Sleek "modern" designs took over the house while the rustic furniture stayed out on the porch or in the backyard.

It was common in motion pictures from the thirties onward to use rustic furniture as an icon for dumb, poor, quaint, rural folk. (If you look closely at early episodes of the television show "Lassie," you can spot rustic pieces on the porches of "old-timers.") Rustic furniture was something you made up when you "couldn't afford no better." Antique shops would happily sell rustic furniture for next to nothing. Many very fine rustic collections were put together in the fifties and sixties by people with a great deal of foresight and very little cash.

In the sixties, as rebellion against the Vietnam War and the military-industrial complex reawakened a desire for simplicity and self-sufficiency, the rustic look was re-discovered. Hippies, proponents of the "back-to-the-land" movement, corporate refugees, and others began eyeing trees and logs in new (and old) ways. They found books by Ernest Thompson Seaton, old Boy Scout handbooks, and do-it-yourself magazines from the turn of the century that offered the plans and the encouragement for making rustic furniture. Visitors to the Adirondack Museum in Blue Mountain Lake, New York, saw some of the finest rustic work in the world. They looked, they daydreamed, and some began to build.

At the same time people started buying and buying and buying. Pretty soon what used to be considered creaky, cheap, backyard furniture made its way onto the porch, then into the hallway, and eventually into the living areas of homes. Decorators and design magazines, ever hungry for a new return of the old, discovered and re-discovered this furniture, first as "Twig," then "Rustic," then "Stick," then "Santa Fe," or "New Country," or "Adirondack," or "Neo-Rustic," and hailed it as "The New Primitive" and "Outsider Art." Before you knew it a revival was born! And here we are today...Whew!

COMMERCIAL RUSTIC

by Ralph Kylloe

The late Victorian "back to nature" and resort movements inspired the commercialism of rustic endeavors. Much later, during the depression years, a number of other rustic efforts also appeared. This was because rustic furniture was easy to build, cost little or nothing in materials, was easily marketed, and people had time on their hands and needed some form employment. Consequently, rustic became commercial and the entrepreneurial spirits of many craftsmen recognized the opportunity.

In the Midwest, six different Indiana hickory furniture manufacturers flourished and boxcars of hickory pieces were said to leave, on a weekly basis, from the Old Hickory plant in Martinsville, Ind., for the Adirondacks. Hickory furniture was sold in every major city in the country, and stores like Wanamakers, Jordan-Marsh, and Montgomery's had huge showrooms filled with hickory items. Disneyland, the Old Faithful Inn at Yellowstone, and the Grove Park Inn in North Carolina were full of hickory pieces. And at the same time designers like Gustav Stickley and Charles Limbert frequently utilized hickory within their arts and crafts settings.

Amish families, especially in northern Indiana and Ohio, also mass-produced rustic items. These people specialized in bent-twig rockers and tables that were sold along with their marvelous indigo quilts, produce, and baked goods at fairs, bake sales, and yard sales. Times change little in Amish communities. Today, in Northern Indiana, it is still possible to see flea markets and church fairs with traditional Amish twig rockers and goods for sale.

In the Appalachian areas, numerous root and twig builders sold their wares at roadside stands, out of horse-drawn wagons, on river boats, and at fairs. They also advertised in many of the local papers, one noting that "country produce of all kinds will be taken in exchange for work."

Along with the small advertisers were the much more aggressive "big time" promoters, including many individuals who advertised in <u>The Ladies Home Journal</u>, <u>The Farmers Almanac</u>, <u>Saturday Evening Post</u>, and <u>House Beautiful</u>.

In the Adirondacks, the majority of rustic furniture builders were guides who were politely told by their employers to "build some furniture during their idle hours of the winter months." Ernest Stowe and Lee Fountain are the most widely recognized of the Adirondack furniture makers. It is thought that Stowe only produced approximately sixty-five pieces of his birch-bark innovations, while Fountain mass-produced oversized birch rockers and tables for many years in the Adirondack region.

In short, commercialism and mass production was evident within the rustic movement. At the same time, however, it should be understood that even though manufacturing principles were applied to different segments within the rustic movement, each piece of furniture was, in reality, handmade and will differ from other pieces as no two twigs or branches are alike. Unfortunately, due to competition from aluminum and plastic chair makers, the rustic furniture business dramatically declined in the early fifties.

Old Hickory chairs at the Grove Park Inn, Asheville, NC.

2.

MAKING RUSTIC FURNITURE

The Rustic Approach: Getting to the Woods

If you can peel an apple, you can make a rustic chair. Creating simple rustic furniture requires about the same coordination and strength needed for normal activities in a kitchen. There will be lugging, bending, reaching, twisting; and then the small motor skills, not unlike paring, pitting, slicing, and chopping.

In rustic building almost all the work involves some variation of cutting. First you cut the wood, then you size—or cut down—the wood into furniture parts. Then for some styles there are holes to be cut into the wood and more cutting to make the pegs fit into the holes.

Making rustic furniture is as much or more a perceptual activity as a mechanical one. The maker often "sees" the chair in the trees even before the wood is cut. The key skill—and it is a skill which can be practiced and developed—is that of selecting trees from the forest.

Not in the last century and a half have there been more forest lands in America. Particularly in the Northeast, where the forests have reclaimed farmlands, new stands of trees abound. That means the competition for light, water, and nutrients is fierce. The twists, turns, and other contortions of survival have made for an ever-rich and diverse forest.

In this struggle for survival, the beautiful winners and the distinctive losers create an abundantly varied palette for the rustic worker. There are the graceful curves

formed as a tree maneuvers toward sunlight; the violent turns from surviving an accident with snow or a falling tree. There are the "eyes" from the scars of dead or broken-off branches, and the cracks and splits from enduring winter frosts.

Then there are the encounters with animals: The sculpted spears of wood freshly chewed by beavers. The teeth marks left by browsing deer. Wood from the edge of a cow pasture may take on the patina of fine leather from seasons of bovine rubbing. There are lichens and fungus and bugs that scar and decorate bark. There are trees whose roots have been exposed after some change in the forest floor and trees who have grown around barbed wire or rocks or vines or each other. The forest's variations are limitless, offering an overwhelming array of possibilities for the imaginative rustic worker.

Now, with your tools safely on the work bench, go to the woods: to amble, to sit, to look. It can be the local park or the biggest, darkest forest you can find. It's all the same. You are beginning to look at trees with an eye for selecting components from the forest.

You are looking at the varieties of trees, their shapes, their branches, and their individual struggles to reach light and water. Notice variations in size, texture, vitality, decay; how the smells of the forest change as you move through it; the scents of each tree; the musty composting on the forest floor. Look at the patterns of bark, the shapes of leaves, the way leaves cluster.

GATHERING
by Brent McGregor

At age 18 I started working in a logging camp in northwest Washington. Through the years I logged in Oregon, Alaska, Montana, Wyoming, and South Dakota. I then became involved in milling lumber and building log homes. After completing eight log homes I began looking for a more creative outlet—rustic furniture. I built my first log bed in January of 1987. That was the start of my furniture business. So in a sense I possess a new image among fellow builders.

Central Oregon is a splendid place to work with rustic woods because of the wide ranging variety we have here. I have collected 25 species of wood within a 100-mile radius of my woodworking shop. We are in a land where the mountain pines meet the desert junipers, producing some unusual shapes and figurings of trees. We have scrub oak, which works up into fine furniture. An hour's drive west we are in the old-growth fir forests, and only a few more hours west we are on the coast, where driftwood is found. I know of no other area with such diverse varieties of potential woods.

I must say that juniper is my favorite wood. It grows abundantly only in two places on earth—central Oregon and in the Holy Lands. With no more effort than walking out the shop door I have miles and miles of high desert country to search for just the right pieces. I can actually feel the mystic, ancient spirit these junipers emit. Possessing a twisted and contorted look, they are ideal for the rustic look.

Being a desert tree, junipers have a low moisture content, making curing quite easy. Often a large portion of the tree is already dead. A few decorative white sap bands will keep an otherwise dead tree alive for years. I use a moisture meter capable of checking 3-1/4" deep in the wood. Much of the tree is under twenty percent moisture in the desert and will dry to nine or ten percent just curing in my shop. With my workshop in a desert climate, drying is made easier, so I don't use a kiln.

Lodgepole pine and maple are great woods to work also. I have recently found an isolated area containing multiple-burled lodgepole pine, common only to the Rocky Mountain states. Acquiring proper permits, I hunt for the standing dead pine trees that have been killed by beetles, or I find fire-killed stands. I seldom try to keep the bark on the tree, as pines do not retain their bark like many hardwoods do. The standing dead trees are nearly ready for use immediately. Many poles that have been peeled and placed by the wood stove for a week or two are ready for use in furniture.

Notice the spaces around trees, the spaces between limbs and branches. These are the images and spacial relationships you will want to preserve in your furniture.

Imagine climbing the trees, living under the trees. Imagine living *in* a tree or living *as* a tree. You will find some trees more interesting than others. Some will seem too big, some too small. You might find the maples more interesting than the ash, the oaks more intriguing than the poplars. Maybe you don't know tree names but still you find yourself with opinions. Those opinions are the true beginnings of rustic work—of seeing furniture in the trees.

There is no "best" wood. Making rustic furniture means making furniture from the woods at hand. I use maple because it grows where I live in the sizes that fit the way I like to build. I use hickory, beech, oak, and dogwood for the same reasons. I live in a well-forested area. If I

didn't, I would ask tree surgeons and neighbors to save me the prunings from their ornamental trees. If I lived in the city, I'd make friends with parks maintenance crews and rescue their cuttings from the chipper. Soon I'd have a stash of Russian olive, honey locust, crabapple, dwarf pear, pin oak, and more.

If I couldn't wait for the wood to dry, I'd find some willow near a pond or a stream and start bending and nailing furniture together. Pleasant desperation might lead me to a friend's wood pile, or to some abandoned fences, or a beaver dam, or to a log jam in a creek, where I would brave wet feet, poison ivy, and an astonishing array of wood beetles to satisfy my needs.

When I first began making rustic furniture, I was living in the middle of New York City and I found that the piles of discarded fruit crates and shipping pallets were as interesting and rewarding as my trips to the woods. The

saplings I would cut in a friend's woods were in many ways like the wood that found its way to the curbside trash in the city. Often they came together in my early furniture.

The rustic woodworker is never ever at a loss for materials. There is no better or worse place to live if you are smitten by the urge to build. Every place is the right place. Many of the home-made antique Adirondack plant stands and smoking stands were made from fruit-box ends, and there is a parallel craft tradition called "tramp art" in which intricate accessories and furniture were created from cigar boxes and other scrap wood. Whether you are walking through the forest or rummaging through a landfill, the need for ingenuity is the same. To make rustic furniture is to gather wood.

There are a number of ways to collect wood:

CUTTING FRESH WOOD. I have several different forests where I cut wood. Each section of forest has a unique mixture of trees—different sizes, different species, and differing degrees of accessibility. It's not hard to find landowners willing to let you gather a few saplings every so often, once they understand that you're not planning a wholesale logging operation. For me, there are birch trees up in the corner of Bob's woods, well-guarded by poison ivy. There are maple and hickory saplings out on County Road One. There are beech trees in Keiko's woods and small-log trees in Haverley's.

Sometimes I use a small chain saw but usually I cut with a com-

mon pruning saw or bow saw. People often suggest more efficient, high-powered ways of getting wood. These are great suggestions if I ever decide to open a paper mill, but for now I can get everything I need by spending three or four hours a month in the woods with my hand tools.

I can "see" furniture in trees so I only cut what I know I'll use and rough-size it there in the woods. The trunks will become heavy posts for beds or settees. The middle sections are for chair posts and rungs, and the spidery tops will be decoration. I flush-cut the stumps to ground level and cut up and scatter what little I don't take out with me. No one would ever know I'd been there.

I cut all year long. Folk wisdom would have us cutting in the winter when the sap is down. But

it's cold in the winter! Anyway I want (and need) to go to the woods all year long. Yes, some of the bark falls off. But not much, and usually only on three-inch diameter trees, not from the little poles I normally use.

PEELED WOOD. To prepare peeled wood, there is definitely a best time of the year to cut. Here in the northeastern U.S. if you harvest wood from mid-May to early July the bark will easily peel off trees in long strips. (These can be used to make friends with basketmakers). At this time of the year the peeling can be done with a dull knife. Otherwise preparing peeled wood from dry wood—or from wood cut when the sap is down—is a long, meditative process that involves a sharp pen knife. I have used coarser cutting tools like the

drawknife or the hatchet but they nick and cut the wood so that it looks more milled than peeled.

SCROUNGING FRESH-CUT WOOD. Believe it or not, most of the people who cut fresh wood don't think of using it for rustic furniture—a true and sorry fact of life. Homeowners prune their trees. Tree surgeons tidy up yards. County parks employees and road crews fight back the woody wilderness. But do they think of making rustic furniture? No! Instead brush piles are formed. Dumps are filled. And there is the evil whine of the wood chipper—that insatiable mechanical arbivore.

I have found neighbors and tree surgeons very cooperative and amused at my interest in their brush. Often they start selecting and identifying pieces

WATCH OUT FOR THE LYCTIDS!

There are a number of different bugs that a rustic is likely to encounter after just a short while at the trade. There are the flying, buzzing kind that sting and annoy. Black flies, deer flies, mosquitos, gnats, and no-see-ums are irritating, but not life threatening. The terrifying ones are their cousins—the ones who eat wood.

As a homeowner, I am vigilant for carpenter ants and termites and have local, friendly exterminators at my side. But as a rustic furniture builder, I am prey to the mean-spirited survival tactics of the lyctids, the anobids, and the bostrichids. These are the infamous wood-boring beetles—the cockroaches of rustic work. They eat dead wood. Actually, they like the starch in the sap wood, and will pass that taste on for generations. They can also pass on to rustic builders a fine, powdery dust that embarrasses us in front of our clients: "Can't you control your bugs, Mr. Mack!"

Getting rid of these various beetles is difficult. First, when gathering, I pass up any wood with beetle holes in it. But sometimes they trick me, and get into my storehouse of wood. Then I see their little droppings, called frass. Or worse, I actually hear them chomping! Yes, you may think I'm crazy, but you can hear them eating.

There are a few remedies. The easiest one is to throw out any infested wood. Short of that, you have to treat the wood to kill the bugs. This is a real challenge. Sometimes I have stuck a paper-clip down the chamber where they live. Sound gross? It is. Other times I have taken a hypodermic syringe, filled it with turpentine, and injected it into the little hole—Dr. Killbug! After a few minutes, they come out of their holes all outraged and terminal.

Some people have suggested serious, adult-like methods such as fumigation in a sealed chamber with professionally-regulated fumigants like methyl bromide and Vikane. I find such treatments terribly "un-rustic." But sometimes I have heated an infested piece with a heat gun or heat lamp, making the wood too hot to handle for the little buggers. The trick here is to not set the wood on fire. If you can get the wood to a temperature between 110 and 120 degrees Fahrenheit for an hour or so, you're creating kiln-like conditions, which will kill the bugs.

Nonetheless, I do have a collection of old fence rails, fallen cedars and chestnut stumps that I can't seem to part with. I am assuming that if I can change the living conditions of the bugs and fungi, they will leave me and my wood alone.

they think I should like. As for the road and parks crews, I keep a casual eye out for them and listen for the roar of the chipper to tell me when they are near. Also watch for freshly-cut trees around orchards, new housing developments, surveying teams, highway projects, and logging crews. From these erratic sources, you can maintain a good supply of fresh-cut and unusual woods. Often the trimmings from large trees and ornamentals give me shapes I can't get in the fresh saplings I cut myself.

Margaret Craven, of Longmont, Colorado, came to making rustic furniture after years as a basket-maker. Her furniture is "twined rolled" and she says her sources are wherever she happens to be:

"The first piece of actual furniture I built was a child's loveseat. My husband had removed a portion of a chokecherry thicket to erect a fence and when faced with such a large amount of material I regarded as a precious resource, I simply couldn't waste it without at least trying to make something out of it.

"I regard any plant that isn't an endangered species as potential building material. I've use silver maple, Chinese and American elm, birch, box elder, dogwood, willow, grape vines, apple, crabapple, lilac, forsythia, rose canes, raspberry canes, privet, sunflower stalks, cosmos stalks, mustard stalks, clematis, Virginia creeper, bulrushes, cattails, wiregrass, sedge, papyrus, honeylocust...I experiment with everything."

FALLEN WOOD. This is wood for the rustic gambler. Collecting

wood that has spent time on the forest floor is often an unsolicited opportunity to learn about insects, fungus, and mildew first-hand. We rustics see trees as part of a pleasant livelihood or pastime. Many non-mammalian species look at trees as one of life's basic necessities (i.e. food or shelter). This makes for a competition in which we humans don't always fare too well. If you can't resist the urge to take home some wonderful piece of forest flotsam, keep it quarantined away from your fresh wood and consider treating it before use indoors.

WOODPILE WOOD. "It was fresh cut. It didn't sit around on the forest floor, so can I use it?"

Never underestimate the survival capacity of insects and airborne spores. Woodpiles are where bugs go on vacation. Still, I did covet and eventually purloin cherry, oak, and sycamore from Chuck's wood pile. I split it all up into posts and rungs and discarded the spongy, wormy bark. It all seems to be OK so far. But that was only five years ago...

DRIFTWOOD. Water makes wood inhospitable for bugs. So wood that has been thoroughly waterlogged is a better (but by no means safer) building material than forest-floor wood. Still mildew and other fungi are ever-present. Heat or killer chemicals can stabilize this kind of wood. I have built some furniture from this wood, being smitten by the sensuous grayish brown baby-bottom shapes. Some driftwood is very strong, some not. The shape and texture exude an other-worldly history to the furni-

ture made from it. Working with driftwood requires access to a good supply, good storage, and some way to halt the lurking decay of this wood.

STORAGE AND DRYING. Finding wood is just the pleasant beginning of rustic work. Next the wood must be lugged somewhere and dried. When I first started making rustic furniture I was living on the sixteenth floor of an overheated New York apartment building. My living room doubled as a drying shed. As my family grew I relocated my workshop to a commercial studio space and my ever-increasing wood collection moved with me, eliciting a stream of comments, observations, and jokes from onlookers.

If you plan to use nailed joints, drying wood is not necessary, so storing wood is not quite as necessary either. The primitive bentwood "gypsy" style furniture is so named because it was built by itinerants who neither dried nor stored wood. The following comments are guidelines for those who plan to build rustic furniture using the peg-in-hole method, otherwise known as the mortise-and-tenon joint.

Dry wood will not shrink, warp, or twist like wood that is fresh and filled with its own juices. So for stability and predictability it is best to dry your wood. Changes in season and climate will effect wood. It will continue to swell and shrink forever as the humidity rises and falls. Drying minimizes these changes. Drying in a kiln extracts more moisture from wood than does air drying. Kiln drying collapses

cells in the wood, while air drying merely empties them of moisture. Some rustic makers use small commercially-made kilns or solar kilns to dry their wood. Kiln drying also arrests fungus and bakes bugs—two very attractive side benefits.

The traditional rule of thumb is that wood will air dry at a rate of one inch per year. So my chair posts—mostly about an inch and a half in diameter—should take about eighteen months to more-or-less "dry." That means I have to look ahead a year and a half into my future to predict what wood I'll be needing. (Nice work if you can get it!)

I have found that the real key to building well is to have very dry rungs. I can use very dry rungs with questionably dry posts. Holes (mortises) in the less-dry posts will shrink around the shaped ends (tenons) of the more-dry rungs, giving me a tight fit. So, instead of a having to be a year and a half ahead in all

WORKING WITH DRIFTWOOD

by Judd Weisberg

Driftwood is unique among scavenged wood supplies. It is found on the shores of rivers, in lagoons, and on beaches. Wood floats, tumbles, and is "wet sanded" on the shoreline where it is found. It may make several floats, depending on rising and falling water levels. The longer wood stays wet and away from the light, the more quickly it will deteriorate. Wood should be carefully inspected to assure that it is sound. When deciding whether or not to use a piece of driftwood remember to "throw it out when in doubt."

Driftwood must be dry before use. To do this a rack that provides plenty of air circulation is advised. I usually figure on three to six months to get the wood suitably dry. If the wood is collected wet, it should thoroughly air-dry before placing it in the rack. Stickers—strips of wood used to separate pieces—should be used and frequent turning is necessary to avoid mildew stains.

In my twenty-four years of using driftwood I have never had any insect infestation. The drifting process drowns most pests. Once wood rots and remains wet, carpenter ants, termites, and earwigs will move in. Any piece showing small pinholes or worm tunnels is a candidate for problems. If you decide to bring it home anyway, it must be isolated and tested (by cutting) to determine if the wood is infested.

There are some organic pesticides that can be applied, but this must be done with care. If the wood can be heated so that the internal temperature remains above 110 degrees Fahrenheit for a couple of hours, all creatures should be killed. Again, "When in doubt, throw it out!"

Rot is often a problem with driftwood. Unfortunately the rotted areas are often the beautiful weather-beaten portions that give driftwood its character. Rotted sections should be sculpted out or cut away if a sound piece is to be built. Epoxy "rot-cure" kits are on the market that will allow you to reconstitute pieces and put them into service.

I am trying to eliminate all mineral-spirit based finishes. I endorse the use of environmentally sound treatments. Boiled linseed oil, nut oils, and citrus thinners can be applied. Pigments in a casein (milk) or water-based acrylic are my choices. The Livos Company has developed a complete line of finishes for furniture and I highly recommend them.

Methods employed by the cabinetmaker can be applied to driftwood, using the tools and methods of the carpenter and the sculptor to accommodate the wonderful forms of the wood. The lap joint, dovetail, saddle joint, mortise-and-tenon, and butt joints are commonly used. Care must be taken to remove hidden nails, screws, etc., in scavenged wood. They will ruin most cutting and planing tools. This is extremely important when using a planer to get a true board.

On glued pieces, I often reinforce the joint with a screw, either of brass or steel. Manufacturers make special threads suited to either hard or soft woods. Predrilling will help avoid splitting the wood. Caps are fashioned to cover screw holes either with a plug cutter or by cutting round woods. Aliphatic resin glues (Elmers or Titebond) are suitable for securing the caps. For large constructions—and with large diameter round woods—machine bolts or hexagonal-head lag bolts can be used. If necessary a threaded rod can be cut to size for extra-large joining. Bolting is the most sure method of connection for heavy-duty joining.

wood, I only need to keep an ample supply of dry rung stock.

I use rungs that are less than twenty inches long, so I rough-cut rung stock at twenty inches and let it sit in the top of my barn or next to a radiator or on top of my furnace. That way I can accelerate the rate of drying. Rungs are dry when they sound like drumsticks—a clear, sharp, snap of a sound when you knock them together. Try rapping two green rungs together: "thud, thud, thunk." Now try two dry ones: "jat, jat, jat." Get it? At this time, ten years into building, I have a very dry collection of very odd wood, and a nearly dry collection of the types and sizes of wood I use most often.

Once you begin to accumulate even a modest collection of wood, your life changes. You get invited to beaver dams. Pyromaniacs look at you knowingly. You come under great pressure to join the local sanitation workers union. The best thing to do is behave normally. Try to organize and order and (Yes!) label the wood collection to keep track of when it was cut. Try to rough size the fresh-cut wood into useable lengths. Decide what pieces are rungs and which ones are posts. Then cut them a little longer than needed and tie them in bundles, or put them in boxes labeled with the date they were cut and their intended use. Organization is the secret to rustic building on a regular basis.

TOOLS

With just a small investment in time and money spent at your local hardware store, you can assemble a workable set of tools for making rustic furniture. Tools—like clothes, home furnishings, food, and so many material objects—are at the same time utilitarian and expressive. Choosing tools, using tools, and caring for tools is a statement about yourself. All saws are not equal. Most saws will cut but some saws are more pleasant to use. Some cut faster, cost more money, or have more personal or family history.

The point is: the rustic experience includes the selection and use of tools. It is possible for rustic furniture to be built out of a well-stocked workshop where each tool is carefully outlined on a piece of pegboard and the screwdriver handles are freshly painted each season. But rustic furniture also can be built from a collection of tools inherited, borrowed, bought on sale, and kept in a box at the back of the closet.

One of the most helpful skills in rustic work—and with much hand work—is knowing when to change tools. As a project progresses, the relationship between the person, the work, and the tools is always shifting. One of the primary reasons for switching tools is to conserve physical strength and to focus energy on the look of the work. Changing tools helps keep a rhythm going and prevents the creative process from becoming just a task. (Later I'll discuss the importance of switching from rasps to sandpapers in the finishing.)

There are a few basic categories of tools needed to make rustic furniture: cutting tools, boring tools, marking and measuring tools, holding and assembly tools, and safety devices.

CUTTING TOOLS

The saw is the basic way to cut. When I became smitten by the exotic quality of rustic work, my first saw was a two-edged Japanese saw purchased from the Museum of Modern Art in New York. It came in a blue canvas snap case and had waxed paper wrapped around the blade. It was a perfect mixture of the bizarre and the functional. I soon broke a few of the teeth by trying to fell saplings with what I soon discovered was a saw intended for light pruning. Since then I have been through many saws, behaving like the great American consumer.

Nowadays I use two different kinds of saws, though I could do with just one: the folding pruning

Homemade shaping tools by Bobby Hansson. Note the drawknife made from an old file.

saw with a blade no longer than eight inches. There are several varieties of these, usually made in Japan and available in good hardware store at a moderate price.

I am now partial to the neighborhood hardware store. I have bought (and still buy) tools from the many mail-order woodworking specialty houses. But just as I build from home-grown woods, I find myself wanting to buy my tools locally. I don't like to feel that I need tools available only from Minnesota or New Mexico through a toll-free phone number.

For this reason (and partly from impatience) I like to wander around the local hardware store. There I fall into that age-old hypnotic state and mumble to myself, "I don't know why I'm here, but I'll know what I want when I see it." I find it to be the closest one can get to induced existentialism outside of audio cassettes or professional therapy. And it's comforting to know, as you commence to build some monument to the forest, that you are employing the same tools your neighbor uses for taming his shrubbery.

BENCH SAW. I need some saw for fine cutting and sizing the wood in the shop. This can be a back saw or a Japanese saw with a replaceable blade or the pruning saw. I use a power miter-saw with a ten-inch blade in one shop and a twelve-inch radial-arm saw in my other shop. The only big advantage of these power saws is that they save arm energy when squaring-off logs and chair posts.

HAND CLIPPERS. These are handy for trimming unwanted

Handy cutting tools: a Stanley short-cut saw, a Japanese cross-cut saw, and a folding pruning saw.

growth from larger branches or to shape twigs for decorative work. Again the garden variety hardware-store type will work just fine. Although I did find a pair that have a ratchet action, which makes clipping big branches as easy as cutting little branches.

LOPPERS. These are the big long-handled clippers that can sometimes take down small trees. They are very good for sizing a tree that has already been felled. The one drawback is that their big jaws tend to crush the wood, so loppers are best used to rough-size wood, while making the final cuts with a bench saw.

CHAIN SAWS. I sometimes use a small 10" gas-powered chain saw. It's fast, but also noisy, oily, and smelly and it always demands more of my attention than I want to give. Usually I need so few trees for my work that the efficiency of the chain saw is unnecessary. But it's available to me.

KNIVES, CHISELS, GOUGES. Knives are probably the most enjoyable tools for me. I own at least a couple dozen knives, mostly antique pocket knives that have seen years of use

before they reached my hands. I love the weight, the worn feel, the oddly shaped blades of pre-owned knives. I feel they are already invested with great power. They link me to the earlier generations of hand workers. An old knife has mystery similar to that of a tree. Getting them together enhances the ties of my chairs to history.

I also use linoleum knives and utility knives, preferably used but also available from the hardware store. Chisels and gouges are knife-like cutting tools that are useful for fine tuning the fit of rustic work and helpful when cutting pegs or tenons.

BORING TOOLS
Making holes in wood is a big part of this rustic business. It is possible to find wood with holes already in it, but these can quickly put you on the bad side of bugs and woodpeckers. So you have to find ways to put your own holes in wood. For nailed rustic work you will need to pre-

drill thin, deep, pilot holes for the nails. For peg-in-hole (mortise-and-tenon) work, you'll need to drill larger holes. And for log work, you may need to drill several large holes in a circular pattern and further shape the mortise with a chisel to accept the tenon.

The power drill is the most common tool for the boring process. All major tool manufacturers make cordless models that offer certain advantages in tight situations. These are fine for irregular use, but the inexpensive plug-in drills are more consistent and they don't require re-charging. A good quality, moderately priced drill will last a long time. I've been using the same drill nearly every day for the past ten years.

Some tool makers offer small, very powerful, half-inch drills. This small size is often an advantage in the oddities of rustic work, and the power of the half-inch drill is often useful for hardwoods. The drawback is that these more powerful drills can be

Barry Gregson's chisels.

unforgiving and wrist-wrenching at times. With a 3/8" drill, the power seems to complement that of the human arm and the drill will stop if it snags on something. It won't drag the arm or wrist around with it, as is likely to happen with the more powerful half-inch models.

The hand brace is a traditional and pleasantly mechanical way of making holes, which may remind some of acceptable exercise. It is nothing more than a big crank that can—with good sharp bits and a steady hand—make a clean, accurate hole without the need for electricity. The brace-and-bit was a favorite tool of the old-time rustic makers.

The drill press is a stationary variation of the power drill. It is very good for putting some holes in some rustic work, but not for all holes in all rustic work. I use a drill press whenever I can. It saves time and arm energy. Also, for my style of building, I need to make sure that the holes in the chair back lie along the same line and parallel to each other. The drill

press is the best tool for letting me control the alignment of the various sets of holes in a chair. But any task for which a drill press is used can also be accomplished with other boring tools as long as the stock is firmly clamped.

DRILL BITS. A thorough examination of this topic could easily become as complex as a discussion of wines: There are your basic everyday types...and then there are the varietals and exotics. Your choice of drill bits will be a matter of personal preference, influenced by your willingness to spend money on spiralled shanks of metal and your aptitude for sharpening or replacing them.

Most drill bits will make acceptable holes for rustic work, but there are a few guidelines: First, because rustic work involves round, irregular stock, a common blunt-nosed drill bit will have a tendency to "skate" around on the wood and eventually impale itself in an unusual—and probably unwanted—place. So for all rustic work, use drill bits that have some little point or spur in the center of the tip. This will lock the tip of the bit—and the resulting hole—into the place of your choosing.

SPADE BITS. These are the flat bits with long, ominous fang-like points (Irwin Speedbore is a common brand). They are readily available, cheap, efficient, and easily re-sharpened. But in smaller rustic work, the fang often goes right through the wood and comes out the other side before the larger hole is as deep as you want it. This might be OK for some builders. After all, it lets any excess glue squeeze out and gives the furniture an extra-hand-made look. (Most of my first chairs were marked like this.) The real advantage of using spade bits is the low cost. They are perfect for the new rustic who isn't sure how much to invest in "tooling up."

AUGER BITS. These are long spiraled shafts of metal with a screw for a spur. Usually the screw is not as long as the fang of a spade bit. These are the most common bits for the hand brace, but they are being made now for electric drills too. In a hand brace, auger bits gently and relentlessly dig into the wood. In a power drill, they behave like deprived beavers and can easily eat up a piece of work. Use them with only the lowest speed in electric drills.

BRAD POINT BITS. I use brad point bits regularly. These are gently-fluted shanks of metal with just a small, sharp, thorn of a spur at the tip. They come in common hardened steel and in a variety of tipped, dipped, and exotic metals. They are being made in the United States, Germany, Austria, and most recently in China. The Chinese set of twenty-five bits can be found in several mail-order catalogs. The American-made ones are available in hardware stores (at a higher price).

FORSTNER BITS. These have a small spur and produce a very precise flat-bottomed hole. They are expensive, difficult to sharpen, and more appropriate for finer woodworking. There is something pleasantly rough about rustic work that doesn't require the very best efforts of engineers.

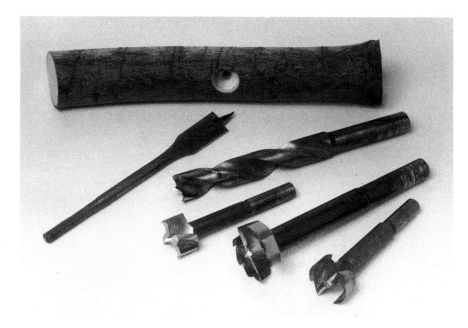

Mortise-cutting bits (from top): spade, brad-point, flat-bottom hole bit, Forstner bit.

HOLDING AND ASSEMBLY TOOLS

These devices keep the wood where you want it until you have finished working with it. A hand covered by a leather glove is the basic model. Here are some variations:

VISE. I have a few different vises around the shop. Some are attached to the bench, while others are portable ones that can be used with the drill press or temporarily attached to the bench. In nearly all applications, you will need to pad the jaws of the vise to prevent marring the wood. In some cases you may need to make special blocks to secure small sticks in a vise for drilling. (These are explained later, under "Maggie's Desk Set" in the project section.)

CLAMPS. I have an assortment of C Clamps and pipe clamps for holding pieces together as I work or for securing them after gluing. But even with pads on the metal parts, these devices often leave marks on the wood. My favorite holding tool is the web clamp, a nylon-strap cinch that holds all the oddly shaped pieces of rustic work together. They are inexpensive and readily available in hardware stores. In a pinch, I sometimes use clothesline as a "tourniquet." (See the "Copy a Side Chair" project.)

V BLOCKS. For the drill press, I keep a few V blocks handy to keep sticks from rolling or slipping while I drill into them. These are blocks of wood with a V-shaped groove cut along the surface in which a round or irregular piece of wood can be held securely. Mine are homemade from scrap pine. I use smaller chips of wood as shims to finely adjust the height of twisting, curved sticks.

MALLETS. I have a few rubber mallets and a few rawhide ones. They deliver a wallop without denting the wood or loosening the bark. They are available in most hardware stores. (Or you can make your own rustic mallet.)

Homemade rustic mallets.

MARKING AND MEASURING TOOLS. Since most bark is dark and grey, the common carpenter's lead pencil can be frustrating to use. Chalk or felt markers work better. Often I just hold my finger where I want to cut or drill and go ahead. For measuring wood I use an ordinary retractable tape measure.

The first sizing of wood is done by eye, looking at the features and markings on the wood, its length, and its diameter to get a sense of what a particular piece of wood could be. Individual woods have growing patterns—yearly growth, the distance between branching—that provide a series of natural measurements to notice. I want cuts and holes at determined places, but first I want to be sure I've visually "measured" the wood to be sure it's the right piece of wood for the use and the look I have in mind.

SAFETY

Although rustic work has a casual quality to it, the danger of accidents is always there. Mishaps in rustic work commonly involve tools that slip: A knife nicks your hand. A pruning saw with very many sharp teeth jumps the stock and clips your finger to the bone. A drill bit wanders off the knotty stock and entangles in your shirt, dragging itself into your stomach. Your radial-arm saw neatly squares a log and sends the scrap end flying across the workshop. A three-foot pipe clamp slips off the knobby round stock and scrapes your shin before landing on your foot. Get the point?

Assume that accidents can happen. Your own alertness is the most valuable safety feature in the workshop. Most accidents involve dulled sensibilities. So get enough sleep. Don't drink too much coffee. Avoid alcohol or drugs. I try not to work with power tools or chain saws when I'm alone, or not at all after eight hours of shop work. Although there is a "cowboy" quality to rustic work, even cowboys learned not to shoot themselves in the foot.

WORK SHOES. Athletic shoes may be comfortable, but they are likely targets for falling objects, both heavy and sharp. Wear sturdy leather shoes or boots (with steel toes if you can stand it).

WORK CLOTHING. Keep your shirt sleeves buttoned and the tails tucked in. Leave no loose ends to get caught in machines. I wear heavy canvas work pants.

GLOVES. For any situation in which you are using a sharp tool and you have questions about something slipping, wear gloves. Yes they reduce your dexterity, but they ensure continued dexterity. (Check the scars on the left index finger of any right-handed woodworker for additional information.)

EYE PROTECTION. Safety glasses should be mandatory when using power tools and are recommended for any shop work. (A few years ago I popped the head of an axe into my glasses and had to have splinters taken out of my eye.)

VENTILATION. Rustic work is probably the least environmentally offensive type of woodworking. Nonetheless cutting, shaping, and sanding any kind of wood creates its share of dust, so the work space should be well ventilated (especially if you plan to use paints or smelly finishes on your work).

INFORMATION. Post names and numbers of local doctors,

rescue squads, hospitals, police, and fire departments in conspicuous places.

SAFETY DEVICES. Keep fire extinguishers, a source of water, and a first-aid kit easily accessible.

OLD, HOMEMADE, AND EXOTIC TOOLS

Once you feel comfortable with the basic tools, you will find yourself more fluent in "tool talk." A knife won't be just a knife. You might prefer a sheepsfoot blade to a spearpoint, or you might shape your own special knife point on a grinding wheel. Following are some of my favorite odd and homemade tools:

OTHER TOOLS AND OTHER MAKERS. I use a shaving horse and a drawknife and spokeshaves to shape certain styles of my furniture. They are nice, old-timey tools. (And they make for great pictures!)

Bob Hansson started building his furniture in an apartment on the west side of New York City. Now he builds in his workshop in rural Maryland using many tools of his own making. As a blacksmith, he also teaches classes in tool making.

Barry Gregson of Schroon Lake, New York, uses a wide variety of chisels, gouges, planes, drawknives, and spokeshaves. But his favorite home tool is his peg spitter—a log with a big hole drilled in it and a piece of iron strapped on the top. The metal has holes of different diameters. Gregson places a freshly-split square of oak over the metal hole and whacks it through with a mallet. A round peg of just the desired

diameter comes spitting out the underside of the log.

Thomas Phillips of Tupper Lake, New York, builds most of his furniture using a low bench (like the one described in John Alexander's book, *Make a Chair From a Tree: An Introduction to Working Green Wood*. Taunton Press, 1978). Says Phillips, "The

only change I made was to mount a cheap woodworking vise on one end and to drill a series of 1" holes in the top for my dowels and wedges. I use a dowel-and-wedge system to hold almost everything I need to have stationary."

Barry Gregson's peg splitter in action.

Keeping It Together: Rustic Joinery

Now it's time to try making your own rustic creations. As you begin connecting sticks, the most important rule to remember is that there really aren't many rules, mostly ideas and suggestions. There are no real problems, only opportunities. You can't really make mistakes, only variations.

As you try some of the projects, or even before you start, consider the ways a design might be altered by choosing longer or shorter or thicker elements. A chair with a double-wide seat becomes a settee. A little slab footstool could be a bench or even a table with different components. Of course you may need to add some reinforcement to keep it steady. Then the type of bracing you choose will make the design uniquely your own. So stay loose. Be willing to change your plans. Let the materials guide you. It's all part of the rustic experience.

If you've looked at the photo galleries and read a little about the makers of rustic furniture, you will have discovered that every builder works differently. So rather than play "shop teacher" I've asked a number of makers to create projects and explain how they work in their own words. You can learn as much about creating rustic furniture from a maker's approach as you can from their plans or techniques.

NAILED STICK PROJECTS

There are many ways to make wood stay put. Nailing is the simplest and most popular method, and it is quite satisfactory for many applications. Wet-wood rustic work, most commonly the bent-willow style, must be done while the wood is green and supple, so nailing is really the only way to hold the pieces together.

For nailed joints, usually a pilot hole is drilled and then a cement-coated, twisted, or ringed nail is banged in. Often the pilot hole is drilled a bit deeper than the nail so when the wood dries and shrinks, the newly-exposed nail head can be driven into its final position.

Nailing can be done with a hammer or by using an electric (or even a pneumatic) nail gun. It is relatively fast and secure but many people find the nailed joint unattractive, associating it with inexpensive "gypsy" style furniture. However there are varieties of nails that may give a more finished look to rustic work. Some nail companies offer a variety of "antique" nails. Cut nails and copper nails, available in most hardware stores, may be a good alternative.

Here are a few simple nailed stick projects to get you started...

Making A Rustic Trellis
by Bobby Hansson

This spring my wife decided to grow morning-glories. So naturally we needed a trellis for them to climb. But in visiting local garden supply stores we could only find trellises that were ugly, expensive, or both. So I decided a rustic trellis would be just the thing.

I carried an armload of likely poles out to a flat spot in the yard and began playing with different arrangements. I decided that the key piece would be a mulberry fork that I had cut last spring and bent and twisted into a big loop with the intention of making some kind of big net. Whenever I encounter long, straight, green branches that have been recently cut, I like to weave and braid them into interesting shapes and then hang them in the woodshed to dry. They are easy to bend when green, surprisingly strong when dry, and can be used for a lot of different projects.

To start the trellis I laid the big loop in the middle and tried several different side pieces until I found a couple that seemed to fit well. I used three short sticks for the bottom rungs and a couple of bent mulberry pieces to curve around and tie the top together. I tried to keep the crossbars close enough to allow the vines to climb and cross, but far enough apart so they wouldn't be clumpy.

I nailed the bottom rungs to the uprights (some on top and some on the bottom to make it stronger and more visually interesting). When nailing, I placed a sledgehammer head under each joint to provide backing and to bend over the nail points as they came out the back. Some of the top sticks were too thin to nail, so I lashed them together with wire.

The type of sticks you have available and your personal design sense will determine the appearance of the finished trellis. But anything looks better than a boring grid of lath strips. So don't be shy. A trellis like this is so quick and easy to make that you can create new ones every year.

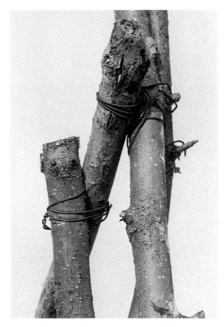

LOG CABIN STYLE CUBE TABLE

by Margaret Craven

This is a nailed-joinery piece that can be made in almost any size. This plan is for a small end table. For a dining table, two, three, or four of these 28" cubes could be used and joined at the top. Craven uses a joinery method she learned from her grandfather who was a farmer.

"I use an iron nail in wet wood," says Craven. "The nail rusts and grips as the wood dries."

Any sapling will do. It's nice to use whips of a different color for the top. She does not pre-drill holes for the nails.

MATERIALS

About 40 lengths of sapling, 14" long and 1" to 1-1/2" diameter

3 lengths of sapling, 18" long and 1" to 1-1/2" diameter

About 40 whips, approximately 1/2" diameter.

Box of 6-penny iron nails

INSTRUCTIONS

Lay two of the shorter lengths of sapling on the floor or work bench and lay two more across to form a square box. Nail each stick to the one beneath it and keep adding layers until its as high as you want it. Nail the three longer pieces to the top and nail the whips in a layer across them. It's pretty simple.

OPTIONS AND VARIATIONS

This log-cabin design could also be used for an ottoman or it could be turned upside down to make an outdoor planter. A big one might be used as a composter. Abby Ruoff makes similar cubes by pre-drilling the stacked sticks and threading them on lengths of wire running up through the corners instead of nailing. Michael Emmons puts a glass top on his log-cabin cubes to create an elegant side table. You could also notch the sticks where they cross to tighten up the form and give a real log-cabin look. And of course, the base doesn't have to be square: Why not try a rectangle, a triangle, or a pentagon?

NAILED STICK STOOL

by Daniel Mack

Materials

4 posts 14" long and 2" in
　　diameter
8 rungs 14" long and 1" in
　　diameter
1-1/2" ringed nails
1" panel nails

Lay out two rungs on top of two posts. Place the rungs two inches from the top and two inches from the bottom of each post and let one inch of rung overhang each post. Hold one rung tightly against the post and drill through the rung into the post. Hammer a nail into this hole and repeat the process for the other three joints of this part of the stool.

　　Now, notice a few things. First, this part of your "stool" looks like a frame. If you had notched each of the rungs where they fit against the posts, it would look even more like a frame. More importantly, it wouldn't wiggle as much as this does. A nailed joint can pivot and wiggle on the nail, as if it were hinged. This wiggle is called "racking." Later, we'll figure out ways to eliminate much of this. Do the same thing with the other set of posts and rungs.

　　Now you have to connect these two halves or panels of the stool. Take two more rungs and position them so they rest on top of the overhanging parts of the already-nailed rungs. Hold these in place, pre-drill, and nail the other four side rungs into the posts.

　　Now you almost have a stool.

Pre-drill your nail holes to prevent splitting the wood.

Splitting seat slats.

Of course it has no seat. We'll get to that a bit later. But worst of all, it still wiggles and racks! First, you might try nailing the overhanging rungs to each other. Predrill and use shorter panel nails for this. Even now, the stool might still be a bit unsteady.

Now the big secret of nailed rustic designing: Keep adding diagonal cross-pieces until the work steadies up. Did you ever wonder about those fancy diamond motifs, those interesting corner braces, and that twisted, rooty decoration commonly found on rustic furniture? They're

functional! They stop the racking. To stiffen a joint, a diagonal piece must be added into the structure between the horizontal and vertical members. This necessary combination of right-angled joints and diagonals explains many of the "traditional" designs of rustic furniture.

All the stool needs now is a top. For a soft, sitting seat you could weave rope or rags or shaker tape across the top four rungs, but this seems more like a step stool, so I've chosen a hard seat. I found a 2" thick plank with fairly straight grain and split off three slats using an axe and mallet. These were whittled smooth, rounded slightly, and nailed to the top rungs.

OPTIONS AND VARIATIONS
This basic "stick box" arrangement can be used for any number of things. Make the posts longer and add more diagonals to make a tall stool or an end

table. Increase the size of the top and you could have a bench or a coffee table. Extend two of the posts to form a back and you have a chair...but more on that later.

ALTERNATIVES TO THE NAIL FOR WET-WOOD JOINTS
Other fasteners can be used if you want to avoid nails. The most easily available is the drywall screw. These can be countersunk and the holes plugged to hide the screw heads. Stove bolts, lag bolts, and carriage bolts can be used to give a more constructed look to furniture. These are commonly used in building outdoor rustic furniture. Both of these fastening methods squeeze and hold the wood together more tightly than nails, but some pivoting or racking may remain. So you may need to add diagonals. Or if the joining area is large enough you can use more than one fastener per joint.

Use a drill bit one size smaller than your nail.

Common fasteners for larger pieces: stove bolt, carriage bolt, lag screws, drywall screws.

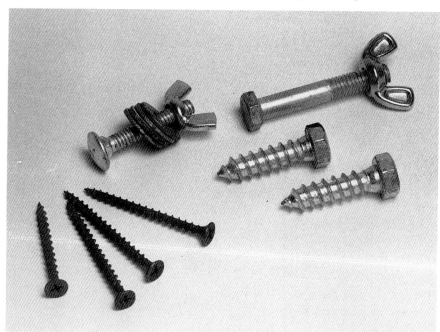

Nailed Split-Wood Mosaic

A limitless world of expression opens to the imaginative rustic builder when nailed sticks are used for embellishment rather than structure. Using split sticks as surface decoration probably originated in nineteenth century England, where it was a popular motif for garden furnishings. Some of the most refined examples of traditional Adirondack rustic work are the intricate mosaic tables and bark-covered, split-wood trimmed cabinetry created by Ernest Stowe and others.

We'll begin with two smaller projects to give you the hang of the process and few design possibilities. In a later project you will see just how far you can take mosaic work. Once you learn to split and apply the twigs, any flat surface—table tops and edges, chair backs, picture frames—offers a canvas for your rustic imagination.

Mosaic Bird Feeder

by Bobby Hansson

After seeing some beautiful orioles and cardinals in the yard one morning, I decided to make a feeding station, thinking I could get some prize-winning photos of them. This wall-mounted feeder brings birds in close to the house so you can see them (and also makes it harder for squirrels and mice to get at the seeds).

I found some scrap wood to use for a roof, a floor, and a back. Then I drew a rough outline of a bird on the roof board and took my clippers out to prune my mulberry bush. I cut a couple of thin young branches that were looking unruly, peeled off the bark, and bent them slowly and carefully to match the curve of the chalk lines. Two forked twigs were used to form the bird's beak. I pre-drilled the twigs to prevent splitting and nailed them down with thin brads. (Soaking the twigs in boiling water will help form the sharper curves without snapping.)

The most direct way of splitting sticks is to treat them like tiny fireplace longs. Stand them on end and drive a wedge down the centerline. A hunting knife and a wooden mallet work well, once you get the knack of holding the stick and knife in one hand. If you grow fond of this type of work you might want to construct a lever-action twig splitter like the one shown. An old machete with a hole drilled into the end of the blade works well. The blade can be bolted at various heights for different sized sticks. Shims can be placed under the twigs for fine adjustment.

Some twigs will have twisted grain and won't split straight. These must be sawed with a fine-toothed saw such as a coping saw, a Japanese saw, or a gentleman's saw. It is possible—and perhaps tempting—to use a band saw for this chore. But band saws, like virtually all power tools, are designed to cut straight lumber, not weird-shaped sticks. Unless you are one of those artisans blessed with more fingers and eyes than you really need, please use hand tools (or buy lots of insurance and be VERY careful).

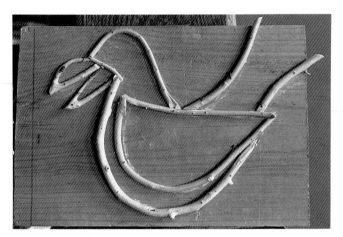

round. I carved some bird feet from a split fork and nailed a big stick to the bottom of the roof for the bird to perch on.

I made the roof wider than the feeding tray to keep the food dry. A split-stick railing around the tray keeps the birds from spilling seed on the ground. I used matching forked branches for the roof support posts, which are secured to the feeder floor with screws from below. The forked cross-piece is pegged to the uprights.

Using a can opener, I punched holes around the lower sides of a tomato can to make a self-dispensing feeder. This feeding station has a hinged roof to provide access to the can for re-filling, but if you use a smaller can, you could secure the roof and load the can from the front.

For some reason it took quite a while for the birds to figure this feeder out. Perhaps the big bird scared them, or maybe the broom-corn seeds weren't very tempting with all the ripe mulberries around. But after a while a few sparrows came by for dinner, so I'm sure the more spectacular song-birds will show up soon.

I like to cut and split twigs and nail them as I go. Since the split halves form two similar shapes, they work especially well with symmetrical designs. I generally hold the split piece where I think it should go, mark the ends with a pencil, and cut it with a fine-tooth saw or pruning clippers. To prevent splitting, pre-drill the twigs with a drill bit that is one size smaller than your nail.

When the bird was done I filled in the background with unpeeled black cherry for contrast. Thicker pieces were split. Thin ones were left

MOSAIC BIRDHOUSE

by Bobby Hansson

Completing the basic structure.

Browsing through my stick collection one morning, I found a nice three-forked branch that gave me an idea for a rustic birdhouse with corner posts that would angle out to support a wide overhanging roof. I found a couple of wide planks in my scrap pile and started to work.

First I carefully sawed the branch into two mirror-image halves. Laying these on a plank, I tried several different arrangements until I found a design that looked right. I traced the outline of the branches on the plank, then sketched in the shape I wanted for the front peak of the roof. I cut this out and used it to trace the same shape on another board for the back wall. I stood them on a table where they seemed to look right and used them to measure the side pieces.

I measured and cut a floor board to fit inside and nailed the walls to it with inside posts to reinforce the corners. When everything was glued and nailed I let it dry overnight into a sturdy little frame for my birdhouse.

Since the forked branch was my inspiration I fitted, cut, and nailed the two halves to the front of the house first. I cut a traditional round door, but it didn't look right so I changed it into an arch to complement the shape of the branches. I nailed bent twigs around the opening and put a slice of black birch at the top. I cut some short split twigs into points and V shapes to create a picket fence along the bottom. (Twig splitting is described in detail in the previous project.) As a finishing touch I drilled a 1/2" hole and put a forked stick in it for a doorstep perch.

The peaked shape of the back wall suggested a star, which I decided to do in a mosaic of straight twigs. I chalked a rough outline on the board, nailed on some big split sticks to form the star pattern, and filled it in with smaller peeled sticks, working symmetrically and at different angles in the adjoining sections.

For the sides of the birdhouse I first framed the outside with split sticks. Then I split a curved stick, nailed it on to form an X shape and filled the spaces with peeled

Elements were chosen to complement the split branch.

Split twigs used to form a star on the back.

127

twigs of various sizes, working symmetrically and making line patterns with the nail heads.

Using the original forked branch as a guide I marked and cut the two roof halves out of thin plywood. I glued and nailed a square center beam at the peak and added smaller notched pieces further down the plywood to fit around the vertical corner posts. This way the roof fits snugly and can be removed for cleaning.

I have always liked the look of tiled roofs and was tempted to get some clay to make miniature tiles for the birdhouse roof. Then I remembered the stack of bamboo poles I got from a tree company that was cutting a right-of-way through a bamboo thicket. (I get a lot of free wood from tree surgeons. This saves me from cutting live trees, which I don't like to do.)

I cut lengths of bamboo just inside the knuckles, then sawed them in half lengthwise. I drilled nail holes on one end and fastened them to the roof. The outside one, which overhangs the plywood, had to be wired on. The first layer of bamboo was nailed on with the open side up—like a gutter—to catch rain as it runs off the overlapping domed layer. To cover the peak joint I split a one-pound coffee can, rolled the edges under, and nailed it on.

I really like the way the bamboo roof looks on this birdhouse, but there are numerous other ways to do it. You can use cut-down roof shingles or make a thatched roof. Dan Mack once made a birdhouse with a roof made from automobile license plates. I've also seen a beautiful roof made of flattened bottle-cap "shingles."

As you can see from the photo, the birdhouse is mounted on a five-pronged limb. I drilled a 1-1/2" diameter hole halfway through the floor and cut a tenon on the center post to fit into it. The branches were trimmed to support the four corners (leveling techniques are described in the "Fork Stool" project). A screw down through the floor and into the center post holds the birdhouse in place, while the branches keep it level and prevent wiggling.

Roof "rafters" cut to fit the corner posts.

The completed back.

Another split branch anchors the side design.

Bamboo shingles make a dry roof.

MAKING MORTISE & TENON JOINTS

The "peg in the hole" is the most "professional" form of joinery commonly used in rustic work. Here, using a very dry piece of wood, a tenon (or peg) is cut either round or square and fitted exactly into a mortise (or hole) of the same size. But complications can arise when the mortise and tenon are not quite dry and stable. If a wet tenon shrinks as it dries in the hole, the result is a wiggle-waggle chair—not much good for sitting.

One way to get around this is to make sure the tenon wood is drier (much drier) than the wood of the mortise. Then as the inevitable shrinking proceeds, the wood of the wetter mortise will shrink more than the wood of the tenon, locking the hole down on the dryer peg. This is what's known as a "wet joint."

(This might be a good time to look back at the discussion of Drying Wood on page III. You may want to force-dry some of the wood you'll be using for tenons.)

The most complicated technique to master in this type of joinery is cutting a proper tenon. It has to be a good solid fit in the mortise. So cutting good tenons is a challenge and a skill to be practiced. There are many ways to make tenons:

The **PENKNIFE** is a perpetual favorite. It's the obvious choice for your first attempts at tenon making and great for fine, careful shaping. It is also terrible for calluses and generally too slow for a production workshop. But penknives are portable, inexpensive, and simple to understand and operate. (They make for great "rustic" pictures—with you, the knife, and the stick.)

A **HATCHET** can be used to fashion a rather crude tenon and is often preferable to a knife for log tenons and for preliminary shaping on larger sticks. The tenons are usually made quite long and often pass through and out the other side of the hole in the stock. Then the ends are often wedged or pegged through.

The **SAW/CHISEL/RASP** is a one-two-three combination preferred by most people I teach in workshops. All three tools are inexpensive and readily available (and you probably have one of the three already). Using a saw, the rung is lightly scored around its circumference at the point where you want the tenon to begin. Then the tenon is chiseled away gently until it's almost the exact size. The final shaping is done with the rasp (or even a penknife would do).

The **HOLE SAW** is an inventive, somewhat crude, power-driven method of tenon making. With the rung stock firmly clamped or set in a vise, a hole saw is attached to a drill press or a power drill and used to cut a tenon by drilling into the end of the stick. Then the remaining collar is cut away with a hand saw.

A few words of warning: Hole saws use big pilot drills to lead them into the stock. For cutting large tenons—over one inch diameter—this hole won't interfere with the structure of the tenon and can be plugged with a quarter-inch dowel. But for smaller tenons, there is a danger of removing too much from the inside of the tenon, thereby weakening it. Also remember that the diameter sizes for hole

The most basic tenon cutting tool.

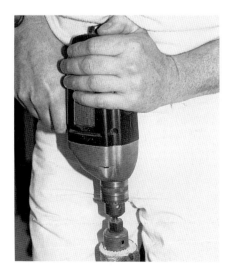

Tenon cutting with a hole saw.

Removing the collar left by a hole saw.

saws are gauged for the OUTSIDE of the resulting hole. If you choose to try this method, be sure to measure the INSIDE diameter of the saw.

The **PLUG CUTTER** or **TENON CUTTER** is similar in principle and set-up to the hole saw but is a finer cutting device that leaves no pilot hole in the tenon. Measurements are for inside cutting, and a saw is sometimes needed to cut away the outside collar. Tenon cutters are available from many of the mail order woodworking catalogs.

The **HOLLOW AUGER** and **SPOKE POINTER** is a hard combination to beat. This was the tenon-cutting method used by most turn-of-the-century carpenters. Both fit into a standard hand-operated brace. The spoke pointer—like a big pencil sharpener—tapers the wood to a point small enough to fit into the hollow auger, which is a two-edged cutter that makes perfect cylinders (tenons) of various diameters.

Both devices are still available, but only from old tool dealers. When they're tuned up and working they make a great tenon and using them will give you good arm muscles. But be prepared to learn how to sharpen small blades and to spend some time tweaking this nice old pair of tools into proper working order.

A **ROUNDER** is an early, hand-held form of the hollow auger. It's just a chunk of hardwood with a hole in it and a blade screwed on. You hold it in your hand and turn it around on the end of your pre-tapered stick. It makes a nice tenon. What's even nicer is that the rounder is being manufactured again and is available from the AMT tool company in Royersford, Pennsylvania. They also offer a type of spoke pointer that only handles stock up to one inch. Most rustic work is larger, so you'll need to find an antique spoke pointer or learn to taper your sticks with a hatchet or knife before using the rounder or hollow auger.

A **LATHE** can also be used for cutting tenons, but it's a big expensive tool with which I have had very little experience. When I have made tenons on a spring pole lathe, the results were quite acceptable. Some rustics tighten the chuck of a lathe onto their hollow auger and walk into it, rung in hand. (I've heard stories of hollow augers catapulting sticks through barn roofs.)

The **ELECTRIC TENON CUTTER** is probably beyond the requirements (or budget) of the recreational rustic maker, but it is what I currently use to cut my tenons. For a substantial outlay of money I now have a motor-driven device with a cast-iron head that combines the actions of the spoke pointer and the hollow auger—just like the chair companies use. It's like a spoke-pointer with a hollow auger attached, or an electric rounder, a whirling set of knives. These specialized power tools are made to individual specifications in machine shops.

MAKING MORTISES

Methods for making holes, or mortises, aren't as varied or inventive as those employed in tenon cutting. It's basically just a sharp drill bit in a hand brace or power drill. I've outlined these devices in the tools section.

USING THE MORTISE AND TENON: STOOLS, BENCHES, TABLES

Now let's make something else. The projects that follow are opportunities for learning about the properties of rustic wood: the surfaces, the grains, and the way the wood cuts with knives, saws, and drill bits. The first project is largely an exercise in cutting tenons and drilling mortises. Then you will begin drilling mortises into sticks and learn about the panel approach to assembly. The later projects will further broaden your vocabulary of rustic techniques.

The spoke pointer and hollow auger.

My electric tenon cutter.

QUICK SLAB STOOL

by Daniel Mack

MATERIALS

Length of solid board about 12"
long, 7" wide, and 2" thick
(these can often be found as
"cut-offs" in woodworking
shops, lumber yards, and
sawmills.)
4 sticks (legs) about 9" X 1"
Glue

INSTRUCTIONS

Decide which face of the board
you want to be the top. Flip it over
and put marks 1-1/2" in from each
of the four corners. With the board
secured, drill holes at these marks
using a 3/4" drill bit. Make the
holes 1" deep.

   Whittle the ends of the four legs
so there is a round peg 3/4" in
diameter and 1" long. Take care
not to make the pegs too small or
too tapered. The ideal tenon is a
cylinder just the right size. A good
fit squeaks when it goes together.
After it all squeaks, glue the pegs
in the holes. Lightly sand the stool
frame, scrape off any excess glue
and wipe a rag dampened with a
mixture of boiled linseed oil and
turpentine. Wipe off any excess oil.

OPTIONS AND VARIATIONS

Make it longer, taller, deeper, or
into a bench, a high stool, or even
a table. Paint the top, paint the rustic legs and then sand them for an
antique look. Or you can glue bark
to the edge of the stool and uphol-
ster the top. To get a more secure
fit, you can peg the legs from the
top. To do this, drill the mortise
holes all the way through the top,
make the tenons long enough to
be sanded flush, and drive a

wedge into the end of each
exposed tenon. To avoid splitting
the top, make sure the wedges are
put in perpendicular to the way the
top grain is running.

QUICK STICK STOOL

by Daniel Mack

The Panel Approach

Every one of the makers I know
builds differently. Some begin with
all the wood in a pile, assembling
the piece one stick at a time. I build
in panels. I assemble one side, glue
it up, let it dry and then that set of
parts becomes just ONE part in the
next step. I try to work with as few
parts as possible at any one time.

It's a very helpful technique for
maintaining a balance between the
elements of a chair. Here's a project
that will introduce you to the basic
techniques of stick chairmaking.

Step One: Two Side Panels

MATERIALS

4 posts 5" x 2"
2 rungs 9" x 1"

Look through your available wood
and choose straight sections for all
the parts. Square the ends on the
posts and rungs at the correct
lengths. Mark each of the posts at
4" from the bottom end. With the
wood secured, drill a hole 3/4" in
diameter, 1" deep. Whittle the ends
of the two rungs so there is a
round peg 3/4" in diameter and 1"
long. Take care not to make the
peg too small or too tapered. The
ideal tenon is a cylinder with parallel sides that is just the right size
to snugly fit the hole. A good fit
squeaks when it goes together.
After it all squeaks, glue the pegs
in the holes.

Step Two: Stool Assembly

MATERIALS

2 side panels (just made)
2 rungs 12" x 1"

On each of the two side panels,
put a mark at 3" up from the bottom ends of the legs. With the
wood secured, drill a 3/4" hole,
1" deep. On the 12" rungs, whittle
3/4" tenons 1" deep to fit squeaky-
tight in the newly-drilled holes.
Assemble the parts. If it looks
good—glue it. Or pull it apart and
replace any piece that looks wrong
to your eye. When you are satisfied
with the design, all you need to do
is add a seat.

FORK BASE STOOL OR TABLE

(well under one hour)

by Daniel Mack

Every so often when you are cutting wood in the forest you will come upon the fork of a tree that just cries out to be the base of a table or a stool. It makes a charming rustic piece because it's quick and easy to make, and the finished piece has more tree growth than construction in it. Look for the point in a tree where three, four, or even five branches have grown out. After cutting the desired section from the tree and trimming the branches, you have the start of a very quick—the quickest—table or stool base. We'll start by making a small stool, but the same techniques can be used to create large root or branch tables.

MATERIALS

Chunk of wood or board at least
    8" x 8" x 2" thick
A sturdy three- or four-pronged
    fork of a tree or sapling about
    10" tall and about 1-1/2" in
    diameter on the pole end.
Glue

INSTRUCTIONS

To start you need to level the branches of the fork and create the legs. First cut them so they look fairly even to the eye, then stand the fork pole-side-up on

the workbench with all but the longest branch "leg" resting on the surface. Let the remaining leg hang over the edge. Move the fork until the leg hanging off the edge is now touching the edge. You should now see how much to take off that leg to create a steady base. (Other leveling techniques are described in table projects by Barry Gregson and Bobby Hansson.)

Decide which side of the board will be the top, flip it over, and put a mark in the center. With the board secured, drill a hole in the center with a 3/4" bit about one inch deep. Whittle the end of the pole so there is a round peg 3/4" in diameter and 1" long. Take care not to make the peg too small or too tapered. The ideal is a cylinder just the right size. A good fit squeaks when it goes together. After it all squeaks, glue the peg in the hole.

To get a more secure fit, you can peg the supporting pole from the top. To do this, drill the hole all the way through the top and drive a wedge into the end of the exposed tenon. To avoid splitting the top, make sure the wedge is put in perpendicular to the way the top grain is running.

Far left: Levelling the legs.

Left: Drilling a mortise.

Rustic designs are as varied as rustic makers. Here's an entirely different approach to building a stool using the same techniques you have learned so far, along with a few new ones.

FIREWOOD FOOTSTOOL

by Bobby Hansson

I love to look through piles of firewood for strange and beautiful hunks of wood. A nice, forked piece (or crotch) is particularly inspiring for rustic work and nearly impossible to maneuver into the wood stove. These two foot-stools, which can also be used as step stools or small side tables, are simple to make and illustrate the design flexibility rustic work can have. The instructions for each of these pieces are the same, yet the results are quite different.

First find an interesting crotch. Start by sawing it in half so it forms two Y-shaped pieces. This is a lot of work, but don't get discouraged. I always take a few breaks before I get all the way through and sometimes leave it half-cut for a day or two. Avoid the temptation to use a chain saw! Crotches are extremely strong (as you know if you've ever whacked one with an axe). They also have irregular grain patterns that can bind a chain saw and kick it back on you.

Start with one branch and saw all the way down to the joint. Use that cut as a guide to start the other side, but don't try to saw both branches at once because

the blade will invariably bind if you do. When you get both branches down to the crotch, they probably won't line up perfectly. Don't worry, just flip it over and cut the fat end from the other side. When you finally get it in half, smooth the inside face with a rasp or a sander. I sometimes use those little sanding discs that fit into an electric drill.

You now have all four legs done. The next step is to go back to the firewood pile and find a half-round piece to connect them. I used an adz to smooth the top

of this piece, since I like the hand-hewn look this gives. You could also use a chisel, a gouge, a plane, an axe, a rasp, or your sanding machine. Rustic methods are very flexible and personal, so the final look of the object will depend on your choice of tools.

The cross piece is attached to the leg forks with mortise and tenon joints, which are strong and look impressive. They are also fun to make. Since I don't like to do anything the same way twice, I made the two ends of the cross piece a little differently.

Sawing the first branch of the fork.

Using a rustic adz to shape the stool top.

Drilling the mortise.

Use the same drill bit to mark the tenon, then rough cut, and shape to fit.

There was a natural knob on one fork half, so I drilled the mortise on that end halfway through, and drilled all the way through on the other side. That way, the protruding tenon on one fork echoes the shape of the natural protrusion on the other.

After the holes were drilled, I held the three pieces together so they looked right and marked the position of the tenons on the connecting piece. If you decide to drill your mortise all the way through, you can simply stick a pencil through the hole and mark the end of the cross piece. If not, just "eyeball" it and mark the location of the tenon on the top of the cross piece. (Rulers and squares aren't much help when nothing is flat or straight.)

Once you've established the position of the tenon, use the drill bit to lightly mark its size and shape on the end. Saw off the end of the cross piece, leaving plenty of excess wood around tenon mark. Then use a chisel and rasp to start rounding the tenon. The trick is to take off just

a little at a time, then measure and fit, measure and fit. Remember, if you go too far, it's hard to put wood back on. For the final shaping and fitting, I use a strip of belt-sander paper in a back-and-forth, "shoe-shine" motion.

When you can fit the pieces together, stand the half stool up and twist the cross piece until it's level (or at the angle you want) and trace the outline onto the inside face of the forked piece. Pull it apart and chop straight down along the line with a 1/2" chisel and clean out the center to a depth of about 1/4". This will allow the pieces to seat together, forming an attractive and very sturdy joint.

Make the tenon on the other end and you're almost done. I hate to use glue, so I generally drill a couple 1/4" holes and use dowels to peg the joints so they can't pull apart. Sometimes I drill a smaller hole and use an iron peg (otherwise known as a nail). Finally, trim the legs so it sits flat, apply whatever finish you like, and you're done.

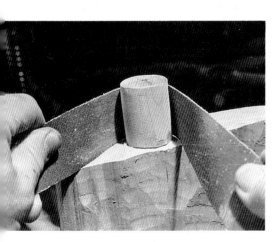

Use a strip of sandpaper to "shoeshine" the final shape.

To cut the notch, first chisel straight down.

Chisel out to a depth of 1/4".

BARRY GREGSON TABLE

Barry Gregson of Schroon Lake, New York, has developed a basic rustic coffee table that is sturdy and simple to build, yet open to a wide variety of design innovation. The simple structural bracing allows you to use all straight sticks or as many curves as you want. You can scale it down to make a stool or use a split log and larger braces to create a bench.

MATERIALS
1 slab of dried wood about 3' long, 8-13" wide, and 2" to 2-1/2" thick (or a log split in half)
2" diameter dried hardwood saplings
1/2" dowel
Glue

INSTRUCTIONS
Round off the ends and contour the edges of the slab or log with a drawshave, or use a hatchet and rasp. Cut four 19-1/2" legs from the sapling and form 1-1/2" tenons, 2" long on one end of each leg. If you don't have a tenon cutter, you can take a compass and make a 1-1/2" circle on the end and use a knife or chisel to cut the tenon (leaving the pencil mark).

To make sure you will end up with a tight fit, take a scrap piece of the same kind of wood as the table top and drill a 1-1/2" hole. Test each tenon and continue shaping until all four are squeaky-tight in the sample mortise.

Lay the slab of wood upside-down on the floor and hold a leg in a position that looks good, making sure the other end extends past the width of the slab. This will assure stability. Place the bit of your drill against the positioned leg at the desired angle, drop the leg, move the bit into position (maintaining the angle) and drill a 1-1/2" diameter hole almost (but not quite) all the way through the slab.

Drive the leg tenon just far enough into the slab to hold it in position. Using the first leg as a visual reference, repeat the process with the other three legs. Then remove the legs, apply glue to the tenons and inside the holes, and drive the legs tight.

Using a coping saw, cut horizontal braces from the same size stock, forming a curve on each end that matches the diameter and fits the angle of the legs. Position the braces at the de-sired height (parallel to the slab). Using a 1/2"

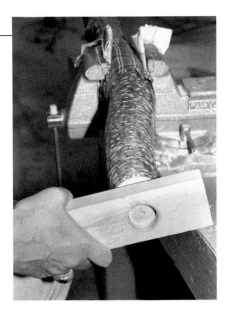

Checking the fit with scrap wood.

bit, drill through each leg into the ends of the braces. Fasten the braces to the legs with glue and 1/2" pegs.

Add the diagonal braces by cutting curves at one end (to fit the leg braces) and flat angles at the other (to fit against the bottom of the table). Then drill, glue, and peg the braces in place.

Place the table upright on the floor and add wooden shims under the shorter legs until the top is level. Measure from the floor to the base of the shortest leg. Then mark the other legs at that distance up from the floor and trim the legs. Bevel the edges of the cuts with a chisel. Sand the top of the bench smooth and apply whatever finish you desire.

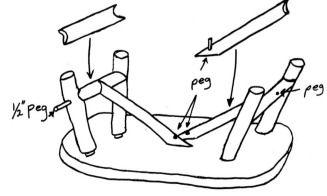

IN SEARCH OF DAPHNE: MAKING THE RUSTIC CHAIR

Ah, the rustic chair: The point where tree meets body, where the limbs of a tree become the arms of a chair, where the trunk of the tree merges with the trunk of man, where molecules are exchanged.

Rustic chairmakers are engaged in a futile attempt to reverse a great moment in classical Greek mythology. According to legend Apollo, the god of music and medicine, fell madly in love with the beautiful nymph Daphne, daughter of the river god Peneius. Apollo was consumed with desire for Daphne, but she refused his attentions. She fled into the mountains with love-struck Apollo in hot pur-

suit. As he was about to overtake Daphne, she implored her father to protect her. He agreed and changed her into a laurel tree, which forever after became Apollo's sacred tree and emblem.

Since they first began fiddling with sticks, rustic chairmakers have been trying to release the beautiful nymph from the tree: the arms, the legs, a back, a front. Every chair is a combination of beauty, function, grace, mirth, stability. But every chair seems to fail in some way. Some are closer than others in their grace, or animation, or comfort. But the total, perfect chair is as elusive as Daphne herself.

COPY A SIDE CHAIR

by Daniel Mack (and friends)

I've been teaching workshops in making rustic furniture since 1986. It's a comfortable way to introduce the novice to the unexpected challenges of design and building. The ten or fifteen people involved in each workshop create a supportive, family-like environment. Here we have a typical workshop project in which the participants built stick chairs using one of mine as a guide. After looking and looking at pictures of different kinds of rustic chairs and looking at the available wood, members of the class decided to build a rustic side chair. None of them were interested in designing their own chair from scratch, so they used one of my basic sets of proportions:

Back: 2 posts, 42" high with holes
    drilled at 6", 15", 18", and 39"
4 rungs, 17" long
Front: 2 posts, 20" high with

holes drilled at 6", and 16"
2 rungs, 19" long
Sides: 4 rungs, 17" long

Rustic making calls for a certain amount of improvisation, but after choosing your wood, you can develop a basic idea of what the final chair may look like. In this workshop, most people made a sketch.

These chairs were built using the same three-step panel method described in the "Little Chair" project. First, a back panel was built and glued together, then a front panel was built and glued together. Finally, the two panels were attached with side rungs. After the wood was chosen and laid out, holes were drilled in at set heights (noted above). Some people clamped their wood in a vise and made their mortises with an electric drill while others used a drill press.

The most challenging part of the process is making good, strong tenons on the ends of the rungs. These should be perfectly round cylinders, the same size as the hole into which they will fit. In this workshop, most people used the spoke pointer and the hollow auger. The spoke pointer sharpens the end of the rung, so it fits into the end of the hollow auger, which shapes the tenon. (Other methods for cutting tenons are described on page 129)

After the four rungs are cut for the back, the chair is "dry assembled" (without glue) to see how things look. This is a vital step in the chairmaking process. Here for the first time you can see how a chair is going to emerge from your pile of sticks. It's important at this point to examine the chair back. Does it look the way you planned in your drawing? If so, do you like it? If not, what can you do to make it look better?

One alteration frequently made at this point is to change the size of the rungs to make them thinner or fatter in diameter. Sometimes the rungs are made longer or shorter. Or you can even replace one of the back posts. One of the beauties of rustic making is that mistakes and ongoing changes in design do not involve additional expense—they're just a matter of time.

Once the back is acceptable, it is glued up. Use a little glue in the hole and a little glue on the tenon. Dip the tenon in sawdust if it is too loose in the hole. Most carpenters' glues—the white or yellow glues—need pressure to set. I normally use a web clamp or a bar clamp, but in the work-

Right: Checking for just the right look.

Below right: A simple string tourniquet.

shop we made simple tourniquets from clothesline.

The back is now set aside to dry—ideally overnight—and the front panel is constructed in the same way. Then the rungs are made for the sides. When the front is also glued and dry, both panels are laid out and holes drilled in them for the side rungs. The seat of this chair is a trapezoid, so the holes for the sides do not go in at right angles. The holes in the front point slightly inward and the holes in the back point slightly outward.

After the holes are drilled, the rungs are dry-fitted and any adjustments are made. After all this, the sides are glued up, strapped, and left to dry. When the chair has dried, it gets a light sanding with 150-grit sandpaper to take off any dirt and to open up the bark. Then a coat of boiled linseed oil mixed with turpentine is wiped all over the

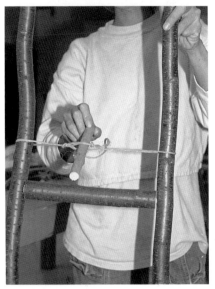

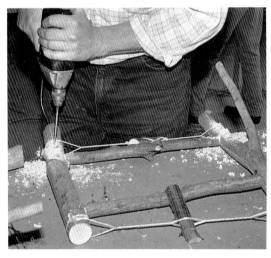

Above: Drilling mortises for the side rungs.

Left: Grinding a tenon with the hollow auger.

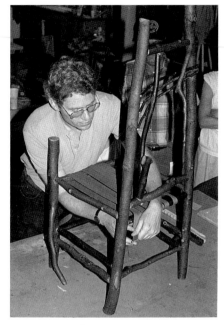

Top: Using web clamps to secure a chair back.

Below: Daniel Mack weaving a Shaker tape seat.

chair and the dark rich colors emerge from the dusty pale bark.

Even when all the participants use the same chair as a model, their finished chairs are as different as the people who made them.

FINISHING AND SEATING RUSTIC WORK

Once the basic rustic frame is joined together, it's still little more than a pile of sticks. It is in the finishing and seating that the crooked sticks take on an elegance and a beauty that makes for attractive furniture

FINISHING THE FRAME
SAWS, RASPS, AND SAND-
PAPER. Rustic furniture should have the illusion of being rough and inhospitable and have the feel of a well-worn saddle. First look at the piece. Does it have a nice overall shape? Let your eye tell you what looks jagged, dangerous, and unpleasant. Get your saw and fix the chair to your liking. Here's where the little burrs either become design elements or piles of sawdust.

After you have finished with the saw, you may want to soften the cuts with a penknife or rasp and then smooth with sandpaper or a palm sander. Then the entire piece gets lightly sanded with a 150-grit paper. This cleans any dirt off the bark, feathers out any scrapes, and generally opens up the bark for the oiling.

OIL. A liberal coat of linseed oil mixed with turpentine is wiped on. The turpentine helps carry the oil further and faster into the cells of the bark. (One fellow I know uses vinegar in-stead of turpentine

in a sort of a rustic salad dressing). The oil mixture fills up the dry bark and helps to stabilize it after the oil hardens.

Almost any oil will do. I have used walnut oil on children's chairs because it is non-toxic and doesn't turn rancid before it dries. I have used regular vegetable oil and even old motor oil, but the smell of both was unpleasant. Besides protecting the bark, the oil makes the color much richer and darker and carries the look of the piece beyond the faded grey-brown look of the woodpile.

PAINTING. Many rustic makers, old and new, apply paint to their finished pieces. Depending on your point of view, paint dresses up the wood or it covers up the wood too much and hides its character. But it does have advantages. The oil in the paint seeps into the bark and helps seal it, giving the entire piece of furniture a unified look. Often a painted piece is lightly sanded back to the bark and sealed again with an oil or varnish, resulting in an instant "rustic antique."

STAINING. Using stain is interesting for rustic work because unlike paint it lets the characteristics of the wood shine through. Staining wood with bark is an exercise in subtlety. Usually the peeled woods are stained, often with very bright colors. The effect is a colored piece of furniture that retains its natural grain. I have used both water-based and alcohol-based stains protected with a sealer.

ADDING A SEAT

Putting seats on rustic furniture is suspiciously simple. You can use sticks, splits of wood, a slab of wood, or nicely-finished lumber such as oak, maple or birch. Try an upholstered seat or one of those rattan or reed or even caned seats. A rush seat is nice. You can even use rope, leather, rags, or old bread wrappers. I've seen seats made of macrame and others that used the nylon strapping found on aluminum lawn furniture.

One of my favorite seating materials is Shaker tape, a heavy fabric webbing available in a wide range of colors from the Shaker Workshops in Concord, Massachusetts. They also offer an illustrated instruction sheet on seat weaving.

Weaving a seat is simpler than it looks. Just tack one end of your chosen material to the rear underside of the seat frame. Bring it up and outside the rail and wrap it around and around the rails from front to back until the surface is full, then tack it under the frame. This will form the "warp" of the seat. At this point, if you like, you can put a foam rubber pad between the upper and lower warp levels.

On the underside center of the rear seat rail, part the warp slightly and tack the end of the material you have chosen for the "woof." Bring it under the first row, over the second, under the third, and so on to the other rail. Bring your material up and over the side rail and weave the top the same way. Continue back across the bottom warp next to the first row of woof, this time weaving over the first row of warp, under the second, and so on. Keep going until the seat is full.

Below: The finished chairs are as different as the people who made them.

California maker Michael Emmons also teaches rustic furniture workshops. Here he describes his techniques for making a bent-willow chair. The sweeping curves and apparent bulk of willow furniture may make it seem difficult to build, but Emmons makes it seem easy in these instructions and photos from a summer class in Colorado:

MAKING A WILLOW CHAIR

by Michael Emmons

TOOLS. One does not need an extensive array of tools for this kind of work: just a hammer, a drill, a tape measure, a hand pruner, a good hand saw, and a sharp knife. It is important to use tools of high quality. Choose pruners that are comfortable in your hand, and that will hold an edge. Find a saw that will cut with little effort. I use a Japanese pruning saw. It operates on the pull-stroke and keeps its sharp edge for a long time.

One of my favorite tools is a little Japanese knife I've had for years. It's wickedly sharp and has perfect balance for my hand. I can trim rough spots quickly and work effectively in tight places with it. Be sure that your hammer feels right in your hand. Find one that you can use for long periods of time without strain. A cordless drill will help you to work around and inside a piece. Trailing a cord around your shop can get aggravating.

NAILS. Because willow is used green, one can only use nails, screws, or staples as fasteners. I use bronze, ring-shank nails in my construction. Bronze won't rust and loosen in the moist, interior fiber of the willow. And the nail heads leave a warm patina on the overall design of the piece.

It is important to pre-drill holes for the nails. As the willow dries, it will shrink down tight on the ringed nails. Without pre-drilling, the small willow wands might split open as they dry. Drill holes just a hair smaller than the diameter of the nail, and a bit longer. This way, when the wood does dry and shrink, you can knock the nail finally into place.

GATHERING. Collecting is strenuous, but it can be a satisfying part of the process. When I go out to cut willows I first look for framing or structural stock, from 1-1/4" to 2-1/2" in diameter. Then I find the smaller pieces, from 3/4" to 1-1/4" in diameter, which are used for the arms, backs and seats. Finally I collect lots of benders, the long slender flexible pieces that create the wonderful curves and add comfort to willow chairs.

After getting the load trimmed and prepared, I am ready to begin cutting my pieces to size. The butt ends of the largest saplings will be cut into pieces 12" to 16" long for the front legs and 24" to 30" for the back legs, depending on the style of the chair. Then from the 1-1/4" to 1-1/2" stock, I cut pieces 24" long for the framing of the chair.

BUILDING THE FRAME. Most people look at the intricacy of a willow design and wonder how on earth it could be done. But making a willow chair involves a fairly simple process. I start by building the frame, beginning with the sides. Each of the front legs are connected to the back legs with two 24" pieces. The top one declines toward the back leg slightly. This helps to establish a comfortable seat. The back leg pitches back slightly.

After I have determined that the proportions are even on each side, I connect the two sides with 24" pieces—three in front and two at the back. Then I brace the frame with two interior diagonals, from the top of the front leg to the bottom of the back. I then place a piece 30" long connecting the tops of the back legs. This piece completes the structure of the frame and will be used to anchor the arms. I double-nail each joint and when it's complete, I'll have a solid foundation upon which to fill in the rest of the chair.

ADDING THE BENDERS, THE BACK, AND THE ARMS. Now begins the process of adding the smaller, flexible saplings. The arms are next. The first pieces go on—one on each side—from the bottom cross-piece on the front of the chair curving around the side that will be connected to the 30" piece at the top of the back legs. After both are tacked in temporarily, I stand back and look to be sure that the arcs on each side are balanced. (It is important to develop the eye for balancing the piece visually as you work. The precision of a tape measure when working with a random material like this can be misleading and may ultimately unbalance your design.)

When I am satisfied that the sides are even, I add one piece at a time to each side, nailing about every six inches along the length of the arm piece

from front to back until I have four saplings on each side to form the arms. As I add pieces, I work from side to side, so that the balance of tension will be maintained. If I were to add all four arm pieces to one side before doing the other, the chair would be thrown out of balance.

Willow saplings are like springs when they are green. Until they have seasoned and the vitality has left the fiber, they have a tension that must be reckoned with when building a chair. Hence, it is important to bear in mind that the balance of tension must be maintained throughout the entire process.

After the arms are done, I use long saplings (7 to 8 feet) to form the back. Working from side to side again, I use four pieces nailed to each other in a nice even arc.

THE SEAT. After the back is complete, I'm ready to do the seat. First I nail three rigid cross-members (1-1/4" to 1-1/2" diameter) from side to side across the inside of the frame. One cross-member is attached right behind the legs, one about two-thirds of the way back, and one piece between the two back legs (about where the small of the back would rest above the seat).

Now I am ready to put the seat together. I use nine to eleven pieces, 1/2" to 3/4" in diameter at the base and 4' to 5' long. I nail each one to the two crossbars on the seat, then bend and nail them to the two crossbars up the back. I usually fan the benders out and nail them to the arch that forms the back of the chair. I use ten different sizes of nails in assembling a chair, the smallest nails are used to attach the seat willows to the arch. I clip the ends and "BOING!" It's a chair! The process is fairly simple. Just keep it balanced and work from side to side.

FOLDING TWIG CHAIR

by Abby Ruoff

(Reprinted from *Making Twig Furniture & Other Household Things*, published 1991 by Hartley & Marks, Point Roberts, WA.)

MATERIALS

2 front legs (A) 53" X 1-1/4"
2 back legs (B) 30" X 1-1/2"
2 back leg rests (C) 28" X 1-1/4"
6 back ribs (D) 30" long, 1-1/4" to 1-1/2" diameter
11 seat braces (E) 7" long, 3/4" to 1-1/2" diameter
8 seat ribs (F) 14" X 1-1/4"
2 threaded metal rods 25" X 1/4"
1 threaded metal rod 14" X 1/4"
1 threaded metal rod 12" X 1/4"
8 nuts and washers to fit the rods
1 wooden dowel 12" X 1/2"
Wood glue

INSTRUCTIONS

Measure, mark, and drill holes all the way through and 1" from each end of the eleven seat braces (E), the six back ribs (D), and the two back leg rests (C). Drill holes in each of the two front legs (A) and each of the two back legs (B) at 1" from one end and 18" from the opposite ends. Drill holes in each of the eight seat ribs (F) at 1" from one end and 3" from the other.

Before threading the parts on the metal rods, you should arrange them in their proper order on the floor or work table to achieve the most pleasing placement. Start with the back. Place the hole in the end of one seat brace (E) next to the central hole in one of the front legs (A). Continue laying the sticks down from left to right in the following order: E, D, E, C, E, D, E, D, E, D, E, D, E, C, E, D, E, A, E. The order for the seat sticks will be: E, F, E, F, E, B, E, F, E, F, E, F, E, F, E, B, E, F, E, F, E. It is generally a good idea to place the heavier pieces toward the outside. When you are satisfied with the placement of the parts, you are ready to begin putting your chair together.

Start by countersinking the outermost holes on the assembly 1/2" deep and 1/2" in diameter so the threaded rod nuts and rod ends will be hidden from view. Place a nut and washer on one end of each of the four threaded rods. To assemble the back, start with one 25" rod and string the parts on in the above order. Force the parts together for a snug fit and thread a nut and washer on the exposed rod end. Thread the 12" rod through the top holes of back and secure with the nut and washer.

Line up the hole you drilled 3" from the end of one seat rib (F) to the right of the remaining hole in the first seat brace (E) and thread the 25" rod through the holes and continue threading the seat pieces to the back assembly in the order you laid them out above. Force the parts together for a snug fit and secure with a nut and washer. Thread the 14" rod through the holes at the other ends of the seat ribs and secure. Cut the wooden dowel to fit the depth of the eight countersunk holes and glue the plugs in place to hide the rod ends.

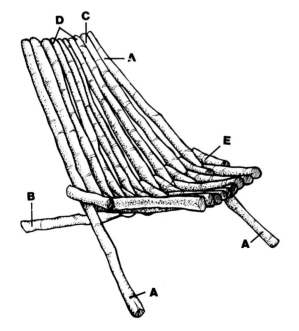

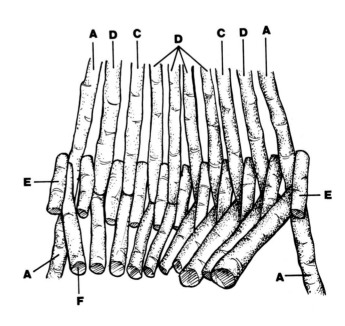

The term "rustic" furniture can apply to more than just trees and logs. It involves using whatever wood you can find "in a rustic manner." In other words, working directly from the wood without formal plans or dimensions, letting the material guide you toward its best use. Here's a perfect example from Bobby Hansson, who loves to do things a little bit differently—like building a chair from a single piece of scrap wood.

BEAVER BOB'S SINGLE SLAB CHAIR

by Bobby Hansson

When a big tree is brought to the lumber mill to be cut into boards, the first pass of the saw takes a half-round, bark-covered slice off the wide, stump end (see illustration). The second cut completes the job of removing the taper, thus preparing the log for full-length sawing. What remains is a tall, rough-cut, triangular board that normally ends up being sold for mulch or firewood. Needless to say these can be acquired cheaply (sometimes free) for use in rustic furniture.

I once heard a story about a crew of old woodsmen who were sitting around the campfire one night, swapping tales of north-woods survival and ingenuity, when the one they called "Beaver Bob" issued a challenge:

"Suppose you were setting up camp and you needed something to sit on, but all you had was one old sawmill plank, no nails, and no glue. How good of a chair could you conjure up and build in a day's time?"

Without retelling the saga of the contest that ensued, suffice it to say I found myself daydreaming of the chair I would have made from this rather oddly shaped board. The result was the design shown in the second illustration. As you can see, not much of the slab is wasted. It requires fairly snug joints—but no nails or glue—and is held together with one peg and two wedges. It can be built in an afternoon and easily dismantled for storage or moving.

The photos show two variations on this design. To me, the rustic spirit involves finding the right piece of wood and responding to it, so I didn't copy the original plan exactly. (The sharp-eyed reader will notice that I decided to make the seat a little wider, so I used another board for the front legs, which I also braced with small rungs to minimize racking.) But as my friend José used to say, "Don't be a slave to your drawing."

I used a red-oak sawmill plank that had been leaning against the woodshed for about a year. It was weathered to a beautiful gray and warped into a soft

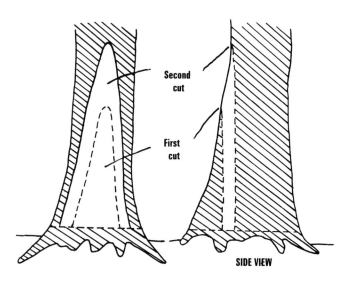

FRONT VIEW: Mighty oak tree, showing where first two cuts are made to square it for sawing into lumber.

Second cut

First cut

SIDE VIEW

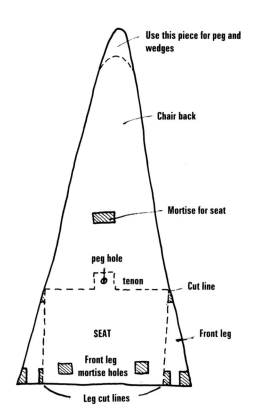

Use this piece for peg and wedges

Chair back

Mortise for seat

peg hole

tenon

Cut line

SEAT

Front leg

Front leg mortise holes

Leg cut lines

curve (making it more comfortable for the back and the seat). The sawmill had ripped the bark off this piece with a big grinder leaving a ragged outline. This I removed by drawing a smooth line along the grain pattern with chalk and cutting the shape with a saber saw (one of the few power tools that are fairly safe to use on warped wood, as long as you wear safety glasses and don't cut through your power cord).

Standing the piece up, I chalked a centerline. At a right angle to this I made the line that would divide the seat from the chair bottom. Since I had enough board I was able to make this a straight cut and form the tenon tongue on the seat later (rather than being a slave to my drawing). For a 1-1/4" board, the tongue should be about 3" long and 3" wide.

After cutting, I leaned the back piece up against the workbench and, holding the seat where it looked right, used the tenon tongue to mark the mortise-cut outline. When attempting joinery with warped rustic wood, it is always better to make the hole smaller than it ought to be and the tenon a little bigger. That way you can modify the cuts slowly, testing the fit often until you get a snug joint. I start with a very sharp chisel, then a rasp or file, and finally sandpaper. Remember it's very hard to put wood back on if you go too far.

Use a drill and saber saw to cut the mortise. Or you can chisel it out. When the mortise and tenon fit together tightly, there may be a gap between the warped curve of the back and the straight-cut seat. To remedy this, hold a pencil against the back and draw an outline of the curve on the seat (as shown in the photo). After cutting along this line you should end up with a nice tight joint.

Hold the joint together firmly and mark a pencil line on the tenon tongue where it comes out the back. Drill a 5/8" hole in the outside center of the tenon tongue so that it clips the inside of the line by about 1/16". Clamping the seat to a piece of scrap wood before drilling will keep the bit from leaving a ragged exit hole.

Make a peg that tapers from 3/4" diameter to 1/2" in about three inches. Flatten one side of the peg so it can slide down the back of the chair and pound it lightly into the hole. This will draw the seat into a very tight fit. If the seat wood seems likely to split, you should drill and insert a 1/4" dowel (across the grain) into the side of the tenon end.

Stand the chair up and measure and mark the front legs. If the seat is warped (as this one is) it's a little tricky. You'll have to eyeball it and resist the tempta-

Two variations of the slab chair.

Cutting the outline with a saber saw.

Marking the center-line.

Rough cutting the mortise.

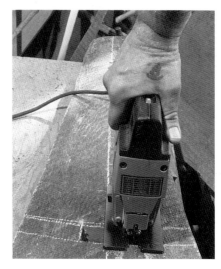

Right: The seat tenon in place.

Below left: Drilling for the peg.

Below right: The pegged tenon.

Rough cut leg tenons.

Rasping the tenon to fit.

Smoothing the edges.

tion to use a square for marking. On this chair I made square joints, while the small chair in the original photo has a round mortise. Sometimes I like to do one of each on the same chair...Symmetry can be so tedious.

Cutting and fitting the legs should be done in the same way as the back. Again be sure to cut your tenons larger than your mortises, then trim and fit, trim and fit. If the angle of the hole is just a couple degrees off (as often happens with bent wood), and the board is 1-1/2" thick, you will need the extra trimming to finagle a tight joint. I like to use both a rasp and a chisel, alternating between shaving the tenon and reaming out the mortise.

When the leg fits properly, mark and trim the shoulder to get it flush with the bottom of the seat and discourage the wiggles. Then make a saw cut in the top of each tenon at a right angle to the seat grain. Re-fit the legs and drive wedges into the saw cuts.

Use a drawknife to clean up the sawed edges and a file and sandpaper to further smooth edges where the chair will be touched. A sanding block or small orbital sander also can be used. Just don't get carried away and remove all the saw grooves. That's part of the charm. (Remember that huge saw blade whirling toward the heroine in "The Perils of Pauline?") Then apply a light oil finish to beautify and protect the surface and you're done.

The challenge of making a chair from one board is fun. And next time—drawing or no drawing—I'm determined not to "cheat" on the front legs!

Cutting away the marked area will form a snug fit.

Sanding brings out the grain.

MORE RUSTIC PROJECTS

Just because it's rustic doesn't necessarily mean you found your materials in the woods or the scrap pile. Garden supply stores sell fence posts and log rails that are ideal for large pieces, indoor or out. Some dealers will cut logs to specified lengths and you might even find one that will cut a mortise and tenon or two. Here's a project by another of my workshop participants.

A "BOUGHT AND FOUND" LOG SETTEE

by Jeanne Epstein and Daniel Mack

Jeanne wanted to make something for the outdoors for a few people to sit on. We sketched a bench with a seat about four feet long and two feet deep. The back posts would be 40" high, the front posts 26" high, the side rails and arms about 30" long, and the seat supports 54" long.

We estimated the amount of wood she'd need and she headed off to the local fencepost dealer. A few hours later she returned with nine 6' lengths of 3" thick white cedar fenceposts, the kind farmers attach barbed wire to. Jeanne cut the pieces to the proper sizes and cleaned them up a bit by taking off the loose bark. We then split a 30" length

of cedar and flattened down the ends and attached them to the inside of each of the back posts at 9" up from the ground. We attached the other ends of the side rails to the front posts at 10" above the ground. (A seat always feels more comfortable when it slopes down from front to back.)

Initially we used 3-1/2" galvanized decking screws to get everything up and standing (and wobbling), but later Jeanne replaced most of the screws with 4" long, 3/8" lag screws. Next we stood the partially completed sides up and laid the two long seat supports between them. We screwed these long rails into the four upright posts as well as the side rails. Now the settee wiggled less and less.

We had saved the best piece for the back rail. We were going to simply screw or lag this rail into the back of the posts but Jeanne wanted a more finished look and decided to notch it in. With a saw and a chisel and a careful eye she cut a half-lap joint in the rail and a matching space in the upright. It took her about

an hour, but the result was a nice clean fit and a more refined look.

Again we had saved interesting and slightly curved pieces for the arms. After her success at notching in the top rail, Jeanne proceeded to slightly notch in the arms before lagging them into the posts. We set a few planks across the seat supports and decided we liked the seat height and the tip of the seat. The settee was taking shape.

Now we had to create a back support. There were a variety of options, both technically and aesthetically. Since we had a good supply of white birch, Jeanne decided to make a traditional Adirondack inspired birch back. She chose wood of diminishing sizes to create a geometric design in the back. Each piece was mitered to fit into its place and held there with a decking screw.

Jeanne said she was going to add a few more pieces of birch when she got home to New Jersey. She also planned to make a seat from the inexpensive 1" by 3" fence pickets she knew were available at her local garden store.

Once you develop a taste for the rustic, there is a bewitchment. Anything can go Rustic. In my ten-year-old car, when a radio knob would fall off or an arm rest would wear out, I would replace it with a rustic twin. I've put rustic knobs on old dressers, file cabinets, and fireplace screens. I've re-handled old spoons and spatulas, garden tools and screwdrivers with crusty rustic handles. The effect is magical. Here are a few ideas for small rustic projects.

MAGGIE'S DESK SET

by Bobby Hansson

Scrap wood on your workshop floor can be a safety hazard, so I keep a couple of boxes handy to catch my leftovers. This is not only a safer way to work but it's also fun to dig through the box to look for useful treasures. The scrap from one project often provides the inspiration and materials for another.

After seeing Dan Mack's rustic radio knobs I started using twigs for all my household repair projects. When I stepped on my wife's favorite ballpoint pen I remounted the cartridge in a twig and presented her with a rustic replacement. She liked it so much that she decided to make a set of them herself. Soon we were tearing apart every ballpoint we could find. (We especially like the Papermate Flex-grip, which has a nice cone-shaped tip to hold the ink cartridge. Twig pens are great gifts: quick to make and inexpensive.

Drilling down the center of a twig can be tricky and even dangerous so it's very important to make a jig to hold the work. Clamping a round stick in the jaws of a vise will crush it before it holds tight enough for drilling. A short piece of soft pine from the scrap box provided the solution. I drew a centerline and drilled a row of gradually bigger holes.

Vise pads for holding twigs.

Drilling the twig pen.

Tapering the pen point.

Then I sawed the block in half along the line.

These pieces are fitted around the twig to protect it while holding it firmly. They can be used with clamps or in the vise. If you file the sharp corners of the holes you can match different sized half-holes to hold oval sticks. The holes can also be padded with rubber.

After she had made enough pens, Maggie decided to "branch out" and make a whole rustic desk set, beginning with a letter opener made from a yard-sale paring knife. First she squished the handle in a vise to break it off. Then she filed the blade down to a more interesting shape before gluing it (with five-minute epoxy) into a twig handle. The hilt of the knife was made from a washer she found in the barn.

The paper-clip holder is a slice of 2" branch drilled part way through with a 1-3/8" bit. The swivel-lid rubber-band box (which also makes a nice jewelry box) is made the same way, except you first cut off a narrow slice with a fine-toothed saw. Re-fit the lid and drill a hole through it into the box rim. Drop a brad into the hole and you have a hinge.

Shaping the letter opener blade.

Drilling out the rubber-band box.

Cutting the lid with a Japanese saw.

Clamp them back together to drill the hinge hole.

Points to be rasped to level the stump.

Levelling the cross beam.

Nowhere is the boundary between craft and art more obscure than in rustic furniture making. A pile of sticks can be joined to fill a pressing need: a shelving unit for the garage, a stool to stand on while painting the ceiling, a lake-side bench to leave by your favorite fishing spot. Or they can be composed to create a striking sculptural statement, worthy of a museum or gallery.

While scurrying to collect the last few projects for this book, I asked Bobby Hansson "if he had time to make a table." Here's what can happen when you try to "railroad" an artist who is known for his "loco" motives...

RAILROAD TIMETABLE

by Bobby Hansson

My overenthusiastic wife was slogging through Artie Johnston's marsh the other day and chanced upon this fine example of a swamp oak stump. She told me about it and dragged me out to see it, wading though the mud and muck, swatting skeeters, and shooing horseflies. We extricated the stump with a saw and shovel under the watchful gaze of a large herd of cud-chewing, methane-producing black Angus steers.

Back at the homestead, hosed off and sun dried, the stump offered nearly as many problems as possibilities. The roots grew down, then up, while the trunk itself swung off to one side: obviously the perfect base for a medium-size side table. And since I am firmly of the belief that time is of the essence, I used a timely theme and conceived of the table as a kind of indoor sundial.

The first problem was to make the stump sit level on the floor. I put it on a flat surface and marked the contact points. I rasped them down and checked it again. After several rounds of marking and rasping, the base was flat. (Well, flat enough.)

I studied the stump to determine the proper size and height for the table top. Using a carpenter's level as a guide, I marked the trunk about three inches down from the desired height of the table top and made a horizontal cut, one-third of the way through the trunk. I split this notch out and clamped a heavy board to it (using the level as a guide).

I drilled two 1/2" holes through the board and stump: one at a ninety-degree angle and the other at about forty-five degrees. Then I put a bolt through the ninety-degree hole and drove a 1/2" peg into the other hole to keep the joint from twisting. A second plank was notched, glued, and screwed into the first at right angles to provide support for the front of the table top.

The top itself is a dodecagon (a twelve-sided shape) made from a double layer of planks. The top layer was nailed and glued at right angles to the bottom layer to provide the strength and thickness needed for the mosaic twig surface. When I balanced the top on the root, I realized it would be an even better table if I folded the back up so it would fit snugly against a wall. This made it more stable and allowed the roots to "grow" out from under the table.

With the top positioned on the trunk, I traced the outline of the supporting arms on the bottom and fastened guide boards to which the supports could later be fastened. This allowed me to put the completed table top on a workbench while adding the mosaic. (For a detailed description of split-stick mosaic techniques see the Bird Feeder and Birdhouse projects.)

Using chalk, I sketched out a rough clock face on the top. I decided to use Roman numerals, since the

The table supports in place.

Planks are nailed and glued at right angles.

The table top upside down, showing guide boards.

The mosaic top in progress.

The beam is bolted to the notched stump and pegged to prevent twisting.

V and I shapes seemed more natural to twig work than the curves of Arabic numerals. After attaching the peeled-bark stick numbers, I filled in between them with dark twigs arranged radially to suggest the little second-hand dots on a real clock.

Because it was already set up as a time table, and since I've always liked the label on the "Night Train" wine bottle, it seemed quite natural to push the idea just a little further and make it a "Railroad Timetable." Though I must admit a few of the details on the train may have stretched the boundaries of twig tradition, such as:

—Bands of strapping metal on the locomotive's boiler.

—Wheels made from round sliced branches with spokes burned in with a heated coat hanger.

—A mashed bottle cap for a headlight.

—A plastic cassette tape box bezeled with twigs to form the engineer's window.

An art teacher friend dropped by while I was working and said that the "bent" clock reminded her of the surrealist painting "The Persistence of Memory" by Dolly ... so I put a picture of her in the locomotive cab, since she makes MY train go, for sure.

RUSTIC TRADITIONS

One of the most inventive designers of stump work was Lee Fountain (1869-1941). Fountain operated a hotel, a hunting lodge, and a general store near his home in Wells, New York, and—like many other residents of those remote locales—supplemented his income by making rustic furniture during the off-season months. One of Fountain's trademark pieces was the birch-stump table like the one shown here. He developed a unique method of cutting the multi-branched stumps to form a level table base. First he rough-cut the gangly legs of the stump, then set it in a tub of water. After maneuvering the table base into the desired position, he would drain the water and cut all the branches at the resulting waterlines. He often trimmed his round and octagonal table tops with split birch twigs nailed vertically around the circumference.

Outdoor Log Work

Once you discover how simple, inexpensive, and rewarding rustic building can be, you might want to take on a large-scale outdoor project. Watch for landclearing operations in wooded housing developments and offer to buy the logs you need. (Most of these wind up being burned or used as fill.) Then you can make your own log fence. Or a rustic roof and railing for your porch. Or a rustic gazebo. Or a bridge over a garden pond. New York City builder David Robinson specializes in outdoor log work and is known for his work in the city's Central Park. Here in a detailed article he wrote for *Fine Gardening* magazine, Robinson outlines the techniques you might need for almost any large outdoor project.

Rustic Arbor: Building For The Garden With Tree Trunks And Branches

by David Robinson

(Reprinted from *Fine Gardening* magazine, May/June, 1989)

Eight years ago I took a job in New York City as the coordinator of architectural restoration in Central Park, where I worked on the reconstruction of rustic arbors, gazebos, bridges, and benches. Rustic structures are built from tree trunks and branches, which nature supplies in irregular shapes and the builder has to use rails, balusters, and latticework. Making sturdy, well-proportioned structures takes an ample woodpile, a good eye, the ability to cut simple joints, and a lot of trial fitting. My crew and I also needed strong backs—some of the park's shelters had posts 12" to 15" in diameter and 16 ft. high.

Three years ago I started my own woodworking business and since then, along with more conventional jobs, I've been hired to build rustic railings, trellises, benches, gazebos, and arbors. My methods are straightforward. I make a rough sketch, choose appropriately sized, appealing tree trunks and branches, fit the pieces, and put them together with socket, lap, and butt joints using common fasteners such as nails, lag screws, and carriage bolts. Every rustic job is unique, but once you know the tools and methods you can build anything from chairs and benches with three-inch diameter legs to gazebos for a party of six.

Recently I built an arbor that used most of the joints and techniques of rustic construction. The clients had recently completed a landscape makeover on their property on Long Island, New York. The six-acre property is

deeper than it is wide with a beautiful old farmhouse at one end. Designed as a sequence of environments, the new landscape is formal near the house and becomes naturalistic as one walks to the woods at the far end of the grounds, where the contractor felled part of a stand of black locust trees and built a pond in the clearing. The clients asked me to

design and build an arbor to cover a curved path that runs between the formal garden and the pond and woods.

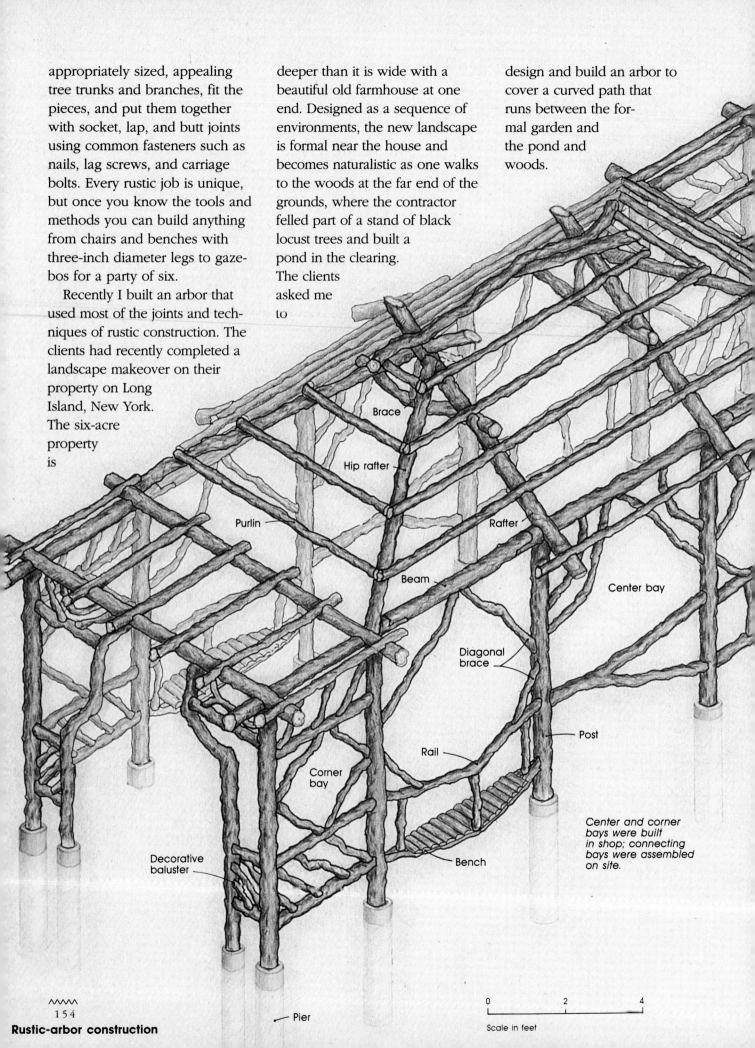

Brace

Hip rafter

Purlin

Rafter

Beam

Center bay

Diagonal brace

Post

Rail

Corner bay

Decorative baluster

Bench

Center and corner bays were built in shop; connecting bays were assembled on site.

Pier

0   2   4

Scale in feet

Rustic-arbor construction

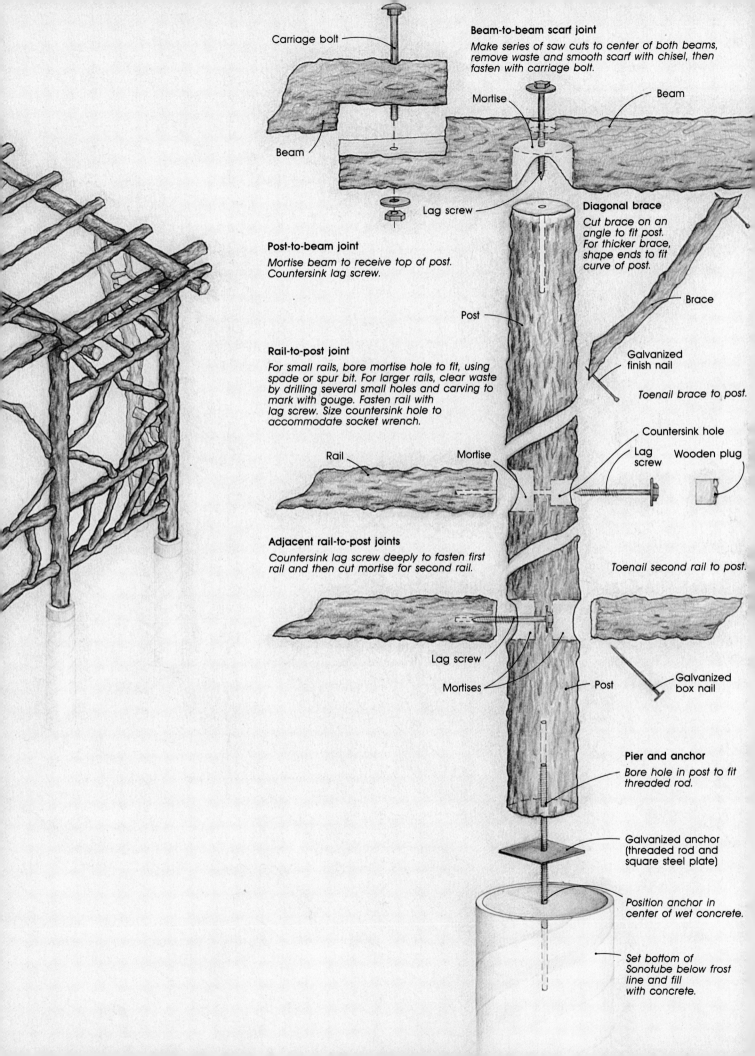

Carriage bolt

Beam-to-beam scarf joint
Make series of saw cuts to center of both beams, remove waste and smooth scarf with chisel, then fasten with carriage bolt.

Mortise

Beam

Beam

Lag screw

Post-to-beam joint
Mortise beam to receive top of post. Countersink lag screw.

Diagonal brace
Cut brace on an angle to fit post. For thicker brace, shape ends to fit curve of post.

Post

Brace

Galvanized finish nail

Toenail brace to post.

Rail-to-post joint
For small rails, bore mortise hole to fit, using spade or spur bit. For larger rails, clear waste by drilling several small holes and carving to mark with gouge. Fasten rail with lag screw. Size countersink hole to accommodate socket wrench.

Rail

Mortise

Countersink hole

Lag screw

Wooden plug

Adjacent rail-to-post joints
Countersink lag screw deeply to fasten first rail and then cut mortise for second rail.

Toenail second rail to post.

Lag screw

Mortises

Post

Galvanized box nail

Pier and anchor
Bore hole in post to fit threaded rod.

Galvanized anchor (threaded rod and square steel plate)

Position anchor in center of wet concrete.

Set bottom of Sonotube below frost line and fill with concrete.

DESIGNING THE ARBOR

On my first visit to the property the clients and I worked out the dimensions and look of the arbor. I set up poles to get a feel for suitable heights and widths. We took into account the length of the path and the arbor's purpose—to guide strollers through the landscape and to mark the change from formal garden to woods and pond. We agreed that the arbor would have a ridge height of 10 ft. above grade and be 7 ft. wide by 22 ft. long—nearly the length of the path. We also decided that the components should be widely spaced to lend an open feeling to the arbor's sides and roof.

The clients hoped that I could recycle the felled black locusts to build the arbor. The trees had been limbed and the trunks stacked in a huge pile eight months earlier. I saw plenty of branches with interesting curves for decorative work, but a scarcity of reasonably straight timber for posts, beams, and rails. (Black locust trees seem to have crooked trunks. Nevertheless I thought I could use many of the pieces in the pile, though the posts, rails, and beams would be wavy. I had never worked with black locust but found it attractive. The bark is dark gray with deep furrows and the wood is dense with a reputation for durability in outdoor applications. I agreed to use it.

A week later I showed my clients a design sketch. The arbor would have three bays on each side and four corner bays forming ornamental entryways. A bay consists of two posts con-

nected by a beam across their tops and one or more rails, most often one near the foot and another 1 ft. to 3 ft. higher. Corner bays are similar but have three posts arranged in an L shape. Bays can be any size. One of the Central Park shelters had bays with 15" diameter posts and 8" diameter rails, and I've built delicate bays for trellises from 2" stock. For the arbor I planned to use 6" diameter posts and beams and 4" diameter rails. I like to decorate rustic structures so I sketched curving branches for braces between beams and posts, creating a window effect, and between the rails I put balusters made of 2" diameter branches, some on the diagonal. I put rafters and a ridge post over the center of the arbor and added diagonal rafters to give the effect of a hip roof. Widely spaced purlins join the rafters and enhance the impression of a roof.

The clients approved the sketch. I picked over the pile of black locust, selected the trunks and branches I needed, and cut them roughly to length. It took three trips with a pickup truck to haul the pieces back to my shop in Brooklyn, New York.

CONSTRUCTION

I fabricate as much of a rustic structure as possible in my shop. I test-fit and assemble the parts, break them down partially or completely, and reassemble them on the site. There are several reasons why I work this way. Many of my jobs are 100 miles or more from my shop, so I try to limit the time spent on site. The shop floors are level and solid. Elec-

tricity is available. Scrap lumber for supports and jigs is close by, and all my hand and power tools are together. And I can ignore the weather.

I organize the trunks and branches in groups: posts, beams, rails, braces, and decorative filler. Somehow I keep better track of the pieces in the shop. In the field they turn into a pile of firewood. For this job I assembled the two center bays, the four-corner bays, two sets of rails and balusters, and the two benches in the shop. I cut and fitted the remaining parts of the arbor on site.

I use several basic joints. On large structures like the arbor I cut mortises in the posts to receive the ends of the rails and I mortise the beams to receive the tops of the posts. I secure both joints with lag screws. Where two pieces cross, as the rafters do, I often make half-lap joints and fasten the pieces with carriage bolts. To join two beams end-to-end I make a scarf joint, fastened with a carriage bolt. Where one beam crosses another I notch the top beam. I fit joints to make them neater looking. For the beams I shape the mortises with a gouge to fit the circumference of the posts. I also shape the ends of braces and decorative pieces so they match the curve of the pieces they fit against. (If they're 2" or less in diameter, the saw cut usually makes a good fit.) For braces, balusters, and decorative work I fasten the pieces with nails. Lately I've been using stainless-steel nails: annular nails for nailing across the grain and spiral nails for nailing into end grain. If you use galvanized nails, buy the hot-dipped kind. They have spurs and chunks of zinc, which roughens their surface and helps them hold. The electro-galvanized kind are smooth.

Galvanized nails are a lot less expensive than stainless-steel nails, but they eventually rust and stain the structure.

You can make rustic structures with a few simple tools. Basically you need a hammer, several good-size chisels and gouges, an electric drill and drill bits, a socket wrench, and a good pruning saw. (A small chain saw saves time and reduces effort but isn't necessary.) I use a string line, tape measure, and felt-tipped marker to lay out the pieces.

I use a 3/8" drill and spade bits to cut mortises up to 1-1/2" in diameter and to bore holes for carriage bolts and lag screws. For cutting mortises up to 3" in diameter I switch to a 1/2" drill and multi-spur bits. (Be careful, though. The 1/2" drill has lots of power and can knock you down if the bit catches a knot or binds in the hole.) To hold big awkward timbers I lay them between two shop-made boxes that are topped by thick V-notched blocks.

Chisels and a mallet are my shaping and fitting tools. I use 1/2" and 1" heavy-duty gouges, 1" to 2-1/2" straight chisels, and a homemade apple-branch mallet. The gouge is handy for shaping the ends of small pieces and for trimming mortises for a tight fit. It's possible to dispense with the drill and make round mortises by hand with the gouge and mallet but that takes more time than I can spare. To cut lap joints and notches I make a series of paral-

lel cuts with a saw and take out the waste with a straight chisel or a gouge.

In the shop I resort to power tools because they speed the work. I use a band saw to cut a lot of the decorative pieces and a small Milwaukee electric grinder outfitted with a flexible sanding disk and 80-grit sandpaper to shape the ends of braces and decorative pieces.

Designs change when the work begins. When I started on the arbor I couldn't find enough straight trunks for the ornamental entryways so I replaced one post of each corner bay with a curving trunk, which made the entrance a rough arch. This gave a nice effect.

Sometimes changes occur because I find attractive pieces. I had curving pieces of the right diameter for rails and I decided to make them into benches to replace the straight rails in two bays of the arbor. One piece ·formed the backrest and I lag-screwed two pieces together to form a football-shaped seat. I connected the seat and back with three uprights, then band-sawed like-size branches in half longitudinally to make seat slats, and nailed them in place.

I assemble bays on a jig that spaces the posts accurately. I lay a full sheet of 3/4" plywood flat on the floor and screw two wooden blocks to it, each with a 20d spike or 3/8" bolt protruding 4" straight up. The distance between the spikes or bolts is the distance between the two posts in a bay, measured from the center of each post. I choose solid, reasonably-straight timbers for

posts and cut them to length, taking care to cut the ends flat so they will stand straight. After drilling a 3/8" hole in the center of the bottom end, I drop the post over the pin in the plywood. Then I plumb each post and brace it with scrap lumber nailed to it and the plywood to hold it in place while I work on the rails and other pieces.

The rails have to be measured and cut to size individually. You measure the inside dimension between the posts and add a few inches to allow for fitting the ends into mortises. I added 4" for the arbor rails. Once you've cut each rail to length, hold an end to a post and outline it with a felt-tipped marker. Drill a series of holes to clear most of the waste inside the mark, making it deep enough to accept the end of the rail. With a gouge and mallet, carve to the mark and test the rail in the hole. It should be a snug fit. Then mortise the other post. Fit all the rails of a bay, then put it together. Another pair of hands helps here—one person can tilt a post and help start the bottom rail into the mortises, while the other adds the next rail or rails.

Once all the rails have been set in their mortises and both posts are plumb, fasten the rails in place. On bays with small-diameter pieces I toenail the rails to the posts. For the arbor I fastened most of the rails with lag screws. I drilled through the posts into the ends of the rails and countersunk the lag screws 1" deep. Then I used a plug cutter on locust scraps to make plugs with the bark intact and glued the plugs with silicone caulk in the holes to hide the lag screws. As the drawing shows, some posts have rails on opposite sides at the same height. To keep the lag screw fastening the first rail out of the way I countersunk it 2" deep. Then I cut the other mortise on site and toe-nailed the second rail.

Once the rails are fastened, it's time to fit the top beam. I lay it across the posts, mark their outline, and drill, shape, and fit the mortise for each post as I do for the mortises for the rails. I use beams that are roughly the same diameter as the posts and cut the mortises to their middle. Then I drill through the beam into the top of each post and secure the joint with a lag screw. I leave about 12" of the beam overhanging each post to joint with the beam of the neighboring bay that I install on site.

Adding decorative pieces comes next. Curved braces are my favorite and I try to find interesting pairs. For fitting the braces, hold them in place and mark the cuts at each end. I cut thick pieces a little long and shape each end to fit the curve of the posts. (You could cut the ends flat and chisel flat seats for them in the post and beam.) Secure the braces with 8d or 10d finish nails. You may have to drill pilot holes to keep the nails from bending and the wood from splitting.

On moving day I loaded two flat bays, two benches, and four L-shaped corner bays onto a rented truck with plenty of spare pieces for beams, rails, braces, rafters, and purlins.

ON SITE

I use a variety of foundations for my rustic structures, including pressure-treated wood piers and masonry. For the arbor I poured concrete piers. I laid out the piers with a tape measure and string, dug 3 ft. deep holes, fixed 8" diameter Sonotubes in them, and set the tops of the tubes level with each other. Then I mixed sacked concrete, filled the Sonotubes, and placed a galvanized post anchor in the wet concrete. The anchor, which holds the post in place, consists of a 12" length of 3/4" threaded rod with a 6" square steel plate across the middle.

The weeks of work in the shop pay off when the structure goes up quickly on site. With a helper I set each bay on its piers, marked the location of the anchor bolts, and use a 3/4" bit to drill holes for the anchors in the middle of the posts. We put up the shop-made corner and center bays, then connected them with the benches and rails we'd prepared in the shop (but left overlong to fit on site). We added beams next, cutting and fitting the scarf joints as we went. We completed the bays by installing the braces, then turned to the roof. We built two roof trusses on site, set them in position over the center bays, and lag-screwed them to the beams. The remaining work consisted of adding hip rafters, lag-screwing the roof into place, and adding decorative pieces to the arches.

When the arbor was complete I coated the exposed ends of the timbers with a sealer consisting of paraffin wax, linseed oil, exterior varnish and mineral spirits.

It's my own modification of a recipe from the Forest Products Laboratory, a federal wood-research lab. It's risky to make. The ingredients are flammable and you have to heat the mix to dissolve the paraffin. You can avoid the hazards by using a commercial sealer, but the ones I know use wood preservatives that I don't like to spread around the environment. I'm not sure the sealer really changes the longevity of a rustic structure but I use it because it might.

I expect the arbor to last easily fifteen to twenty years with a little maintenance. A farmer told me that he put locust fenceposts on his farm twenty-five years ago and they're still there. The concrete piers and steel plates keep the posts of the arbor fairly dry, so they're likely to last longer than fenceposts. The timbers may crack and check but I doubt that their strength will be much affected. The arbor isn't going to carry big loads in any case. If the clients decide to grow plants on it, that will shorten its life, since foliage tends to keep a rustic structure damp.

Over the years, the arbor should weather gracefully. The bark is tight now, but it will fall off eventually and the wood will turn silver. The arbor will blend with the tall locusts behind it, as the clients wanted. Looking natural is the point of rustic construction.

SOURCES

Information To Feed The Rustic Imagination

Books About Rustic Woodworking

Alexander, John. *How to Build a Chair From a Tree.* Taunton Press, 1981

Gilborn, Craig. *Adirondack Furniture and the Rustic Tradition.* Harry N. Abrams, 1987.

Kaiser, Harvey. *Great Camps of the Adirondacks.* David R. Godine, 1982.

Langsner, Drew. *Green Woodworking.* Rodale Press, 1988.

Ruoff, Abby. *Making Twig Furniture & Other Household Things,* Hartley & Marks, 1991.

Stephenson, Sue Honaker. *Rustic Furniture.* Van Nostrand Reinhold, 1979.

Underhill, Roy. *The Woodwright's Shop: A Practical Guide to Traditional Woodcraft.* University of North Carolina Press, 1981.

Antique Rustic Furniture Dealers

Mary K. Darrah
33 West Ferry St.
New Hope, PA 18938
(215) 862-5927

Robert Doyle
Box 565
Lake Placid, NY 12946
(518) 523-2101

Ralph Kylloe
298 High Range Road
Londonderry, NH 03053
(603) 437-2920

Old Tools and Information

Early American Industries Association
P.O. Box 2128
Albany, NY 12220

Your Country Auctioneer
RFD 2, Box 33
Hillsboro, NH 03244

New Tools and Information

Check the product reviews and advertisements in:

Fine Woodworking
The Taunton Press
Newtown, CT 06470

Wood
Locust at 17th
Des Moines, IA 50336

Woodshop News
Pratt St.
Essex, CT 06426

Workbench
4251 Pennsylvania Ave.
Kansas City, MO 64111

Seating Supplies and Information

The Caning Shop
926 Gilman St.
Berkeley, CA 94710
(514) 527-5010

Connecticut Cane and Reed
P.O. Box 762B
Manchester, CT 06040

Plymouth Reed & Cane
1200 W. Ann Arbor Rd.
Plymouth, MI 48170
(313) 455-2150

Shaker Workshops
P.O. Box 1028
Concord, MA 01742
(617) 646-8985

Sturges Manufacturing
Box 55
Utica, NY

Workshops and Demonstrations of Rustic and Country Woodworking

Craig Gillborn
Adirondack Museum
Blue Mountain Lake, NY 12812
(518) 352-7311

Anderson Ranch
Box 5598
Snowmass, CO 81615
(303) 923-3181

Camp Sagamore
Raquette Lake, NY
(315) 354-5311

Country Workshops
90 Mill Creek Rd.
Marshall, NC 28753
(704) 656-2280

North Country Community College
Saranac Lake, NY 12983
(518) 891-2915

Also check current listings in woodworking and craft magazines such as:

The Crafts Report
700 Orage St. Box 1992
Wilmington, De 19899

Rustic Furniture Makers

ADIRONDACK STYLE: BIRCH AND CAMP FURNITURE

Jean Armstrong
P.O. Box 607
Tupper Lake, NY 12986
(518) 359-9983

Barry Gregson
Charlie Hill Rd.
Schroon Lake, NY 12870
(518) 532-9384

Ken Heitz
Backwoods Furnishings
Box 161 Rt. 28
Indian Lake, NY 12842
(518) 251-3327

Gib Jaques
Box 791
Keene Valley, NY 12943
(518) 576-9802

Jackson Levi-Smith
Sagamore Conference Center
Raquette Lake, NY 13436
(315) 354-4303

Tom Phillips
Star Rt. 2
Tupper Lake, NY 12986
(518) 359-9648

Ronald Sanborn
Hulls Falls Road
Keene, NY 12942

AMISH BENT-HICKORY STYLE

The Amish Country Collection
P.O. Box 5085
New Castle, PA 16105

Davis & Wentz Hickory Furniture
New Paris, PA 15554
(814) 733-4640

A. C. Latshaw Rustic Furniture
New Paris, PA 15554
(814) 539-2691

Peggy Yoder
Hickory Rockers of Berlin
Box 235
Berlin, OH 44610
(216) 893-2680

BENTWOOD: WILLOW, WOVEN, NAILED, ENTWINED

Greg Adams
914 East Adams St.
Muncie, IN 47305
(317) 282-7158

Added Oomph!
P.O. Box 6135
High Point, NC 27262
(919) 869-6379

American Folk Art
354 Kennesaw Ave.
Marietta, GA 30060
(404) 344-5985

Margaret Craven
948 Bross St.
Longmont, CO 80501

Gary Dannels
Beacon Woodcraft
307 Kilbourn
Beacon, IA
(515) 673-6210

Devonshire
P.O. Box 760
Middleburg, VA 22117
(703) 687-5990

Michael Emmons
Laughing Willows
Partington Ridge
Big Sur, CA 93920
(408) 667-2133

Faircloth and Croker
Highway 11, Box 265
Rising Fawn, GA 30738
(404) 398-2756

Liz Sifrit Hunt
Box 218176
Columbus, OH 43221
(614) 459-1551

Richard and Lia Ianni
A-Ya Art
P.O. Box 23
St. Johnsville, NY 13452
(518) 568-5015

La Lune Collection
930 E. Burleigh
Milwaukee, WI 53212
(414) 263-5300

Masterworks
P.O. Box M
Marietta, GA 30061

Clifton Monteith
Twiggery
P.O. Box 165
Lake Ann, MI 49650
(616) 275-6560

Paula Moody/Barry Jones
Tiger Mountain Woodworks
Box 28
Tiger Mountain, GA 30576
(404) 782-7286

Phillip and Kathy Payne
Rt. 1, Box 1788
Broadhead, KY 40409
(606) 758-8587

Pure and Simple
117 W. Hempstead
P.O. Box 535
Nashville, AR 71852

COLORED AND DYED

Hermone Futrell
11511 E. Virginia Dr.
Aurora, CO 80025
(303) 343-3861

Don C. King
HC67 Box 2079
Challis, ID 83226
(208) 838-2449

Monte Lindsley
Ptarmigan Willow
P.O. Box 551
Fall City, WA 98024
(206) 392-5767

Barry Schwartz
Willow Works
209 Glen Cove Ave.
Sea Cliff, NY 11579
(516) 676-8397

DRIFTWOOD

Susan Parish
2898 Glascock
Oakland, CA 94601
(510) 261-0353

Judd Weisberg
Rt. 42
Lexington, NY 12452
(518) 989-6583

HICKORY

Flat Rock Furniture
RR 1, Box 403A
Flat Rock, IN 47234

SOURCES:

(Continued)

Old Hickory Furniture Co.
403 South Noble St.
Shelbyville, IN 46176
(317) 398-3151

LOG WORK

Great American Log Furniture Co.
P.O. Box 3360
Ketchum, ID 83340
(800) 624-5779

Lodgepole Manufacturing
Star Rt. 15
Jackson, WY 83001

John and Gary Phillips
The Drawknife
P.O. Box 280
Driggs, ID 83422
(208) 456-2560

Willsboro Wood Products
Box 336
Willsboro, NY 12996

STICK/TREE STYLE, INDOORS/OUTDOORS

Andy Brown
Heartwoods of Michigan
P.O. Box 466
Lakeside, MI 49116
(616) 469-4220

Lillian Dodson
133 Crooked Hill Rd.
Huntington, NY 11743

Jerry Farrell
P.O. Box 255
Sidney Center, NY 13839
(607) 369-4916

Brad Greenwood
13624 Idaho-Maryland Rd.
Nevada City, CA 95959
(916) 273-8183

Bobby Hansson
2068 Tome Highway
Port Deposit, MD 21904
(301) 658-3959

Bud Hanzlick
Bekan Rustic Furniture
P.O. Box 323
Belleville, KS 66935
(913) 527-2427

Steve Heller
Fabulous Treecraft Furniture
Rt. 28
Boiceville, NY
(914) 657-6317

Daniel Mack
Rustic Furnishings
14 Welling Avenue
Warwick, NY 10990
(212) 926-3880 or (914) 986-7293

Brent McGregor
Box 1477
Sisters, OR 97759
(503) 549-1322

Glen A. Monson
Blue Mountain Woods
1025 N. 100 W
Orem, UT 84057
(801) 224-1347

David Robinson
106 E. Delaware Ave.
Pennington, NJ 08534
(609) 737-8996

Abby Ruoff
Wood-Lot Farms
Star Rt. 1
Shady, NY 12479
(914) 679-8084

Hutch Travers
Rt. 1 Box 230
Wake Forest, NC 27587

Micki Voisard
999 Conn Valley Rd.
St. Helena, CA 94574
(707) 963-8364

WESTERN STYLE

Philip Clausen
Rt. 1, Box 3397
Coquille, OR 97432

Jock Favour
1300 Middlebrook Rd.
Prescott, AZ 86303
(602)445-0698

Jake Lemon
P.O. Box 2404
Sun Valley, ID 83353
(208) 788-3004

J. Mike Patrick
New West Furniture
2119 Southfork
Cody, WY 82414
(307) 587-2839

INDEX

METRIC CONVERSION

INCHES TO CENTIMETERS

INCHES	CM	INCHES	CM
1/8	0.3	19	48.3
1/4	0.6	20	50.8
3/8	1.0	21	53.3
1/2	1.3	22	55.9
5/8	1.6	23	58.4
3/4	1.9	24	61.0
7/8	2.2	25	63.5
1	2.5	26	66.0
1-1/4	3.2	27	68.6
1-1/2	3.8	28	71.1
1-3/4	4.4	29	73.7
2	5.1	30	76.2
2-1/2	6.4	31	78.7
3	7.6	32	81.3
3-1/2	8.9	33	83.8
4	10.2	34	86.4
4-1/2	11.4	35	88.9
5	12.7	36	91.4
6	15.2	37	94.0
7	17.8	38	96.5
8	20.3	39	99.1
9	22.9	40	101.6
10	25.4	41	104.1
11	27.9	42	106.7
12	30.5	43	109.2
13	33.0	44	111.8
14	35.6	45	114.3
15	38.1	46	116.8
16	40.6	47	119.4
17	43.2	48	121.9
18	45.7	49	124.5
		50	127.0